# GETTING PAID

*Ensuring you collect your business debts*

**J. L. Spencer, FCA**

MERCURY

First published in 1991
by Mercury Books
Gold Arrow Publications Limited
862 Garratt Lane, London SW17 0NB

Cartoons by Ken Pyne

Set in Palatino by Phoenix Photosetting, Chatham
Printed and bound in Great Britain by
Mackays of Chatham, PLC, Chatham, Kent

*British Library Cataloguing in Publication Data is available*

ISBN 1–85251–058–2

# Introduction

If someone walks into your high street shop, picks up some goods from the shelves and makes off with them without paying, it is called shoplifting or, more simply, theft. It is a criminal offence and can lead to fines and imprisonment. At the least it can lead to you running down the street shouting 'Stop thief!' and possibly engaging the shoplifter physically.

But anyone can walk into your company's offices, request and take goods and never pay the bill for them; they can walk into a solicitor's office, request and receive their services and never pay for them. The law not only does not provide for fines and imprisonment for this, but it does not regard it as theft; it is not a criminal offence, but a civil one.

There are differences, of course; you make the decision to extend trust to debtors, the shoplifter does not consult you for permission. Your debtor cannot usually be shown to have deliberately sought to avoid payment from the outset (though many do) whereas the shoplifter can hardly argue that subsequent circumstances overtook him.

Whatever you think of the distinction, it is there and you must abide by the law. Because the law is –

practically speaking – stacked against you and in your debtor's favour, then it is wise not to let matters reach that stage. Prompt and planned action with regard to all your credit control is essential and this book gives the necessary guidance for that.

If you do have to go to law, then this book explains the courses open to you, and the most efficient actions available. It also covers situations such as harassment and over-zealous debt collection where, without caution, it is possible for *you* to end up in court rather than your debtor. In particular, treating your debtor like a criminal can easily lead you to a wrong course of action, tempting though it may be.

Anyone owed money by another should learn the lessons of this book until they become second nature, and then use them. The alternatives can be costly; of those that end up in the bankruptcy courts, a good many got there by not getting the money they were owed by others.

# SECTION 1

# THE BUSINESS SYSTEM AND

# THE NATURE OF DEBTS

## THE ENEMY – DEBTORS

'In God we trust – the rest pay cash!' (Anon)

If every time a business transaction took place it was completed on the spot, debts would not exist. You, the trader, would hand over the goods and your customer would hand over the money.

No debts. No fuss. No risk.

No chance! Life should be so simple!

It is true that some businesses do manage to run this way, in particular the retail trade. Generally speaking when you go into a shop to buy its goods, then you are expected to hand over the cash at the time. In fact, even in this circumstance, shops run certain risks – they may take cheques that can 'bounce' for example – but in that case you are not the shop's debtor: for practical purposes, you have paid for the goods when you handed over the cheque, just as if you handed over cash. (The question of what to do about bounced cheques is dealt with separately on page 50.)

Debtors are those people who owe you payment for the goods or services you have sold to them. (There are a lot of other definitions of debtors not included in this book as we are restricted by the laws governing obscene publications!) In fact, even shops tend to have debtors; they open accounts for regular customers or traders who are then expected to settle their bills at the end of a stipulated period, usually a month. For many businesses, however, debtors are an essential part of the trading cycle; most service industries have no other way of working. For example, if you engage a solicitor to act on your behalf, then you cannot pay him until he has completed at least some part of the work you have asked him to do. When he completes the work and notifies you of how much he is charging you for it (in other words, he sends you his bill), you become a debtor until the time when you pay him. For this reason the sale of services does not work in the same way as the sale of goods.

In reality, most businesses have debtors for no better reason than that it is expected of them to do so. When a potential customer comes along to buy your goods or services, he may expect you to give him time to pay on the practical grounds that if you don't, then your competitors will; so to keep your share of the market (in fact to *get* your share of the market) you have to 'play ball'.

There are, of course, certain 'industries' free of this credit system where you can rely on your competitors not to spoil matters; the Arthur Daleys of this world are an example of this. As we shall see in later chapters, debtors need motivation to make them pay up – receivers of stolen goods are thought to lose that motivation once the goods have been provided!

- **Debtors are a part of business, not an aberration of it.**

[ 4 ]

## THE COST OF BORROWING

> 'The human species, according to the best theory I can form of it, is composed of two distinct races, the men who borrow, and the men who lend.' (Charles Lamb)

In the unlikely, and probably undesirable, situation that debtors (the people who owe you money) and creditors (the people you owe money to) balance exactly, then in effect they are self-financing. However, in reality debtors tend to outweigh creditors, except in specific industries. Where debtors and creditors have equal credit periods (say, you take a month to pay bills and allow your customers a month to pay you), then debtors *should* outweigh creditors; this means that you're selling the goods for more than you buy them for, which is as good a starting point for sensible trading as any!

For this reason, the imbalance between debtors and creditors has to be financed from somewhere. If you, the proprietor of the business, do not have loans or overdrafts, then you are personally financing this difference by not taking out of the business some of the money you have earned. This means you are saving the cost of borrowing money (in other words, not paying interest charges), which adds to your profitability. When you cannot or will not finance this imbalance yourself, then you borrow from someone, usually the bank, in order to do so. In this case you must recognise from the outset that you will be paying certain interest charges throughout the year and you must remember to account for these; in *cashflow* projections (forward predictions of what is likely to happen) you must account for the charges when they are likely to be payable (for bank borrowing this is usually quarterly), and in *pricing* (setting the price at which you wish to sell your products), you must recognise this cost as an overhead expense that has to be recovered from the profitability of your sales.

- **Giving credit has to be paid for.**

## INFLATION

> 'Inflation in the Sixties was a nuisance to be endured, like varicose veins or French foreign policy.' (Bernard Levin)

Inflation is a much discussed and complex financial effect, and the focus of much government effort nationally and internationally. However, for our purposes, its effects on debts are very simple to illustrate.

Inflation is a measure of the erosion of value of money over a period of time.

Money has no intrinsic value of its own and is useful only for the goods and services that it can buy. In a situation of, say, 10% inflation and where that 10% increase is reflected both in money received and money spent, then there is no overall loss in the value of money. To illustrate this; if you receive £10,000 on 1st January 1990 then you can use that money to purchase two items valued at £5,000 on the same date. In a situation of perfectly balanced inflation of 10%, then one year later, i.e. on 1st January 1991, your prices will have risen by 10% and the sale of the same item will yield you an income of £11,000; at the same time, your cost of purchases will have risen by 10% and the two items of £5,000 will now cost you £5,500 each. You are therefore no worse off because your £10,000 could buy you two such items on 1st January 1990 and it will still buy you two similar items on 1st January 1991. Easy so far? Even the Chancellor should still be with us at this stage.

The problem for you as an entrepreneur allowing your debtors long credit periods is that credit does not take account of inflation. Suppose you were to sell an item for £10,000 on 1st January 1991 and allow your debtor one year to pay his debt, then on 1st January 1991 you will receive £10,000. However, whereas on 1st January 1990 (when you sold your product) you could have purchased two items for £5,000 each, you are now unable to do so on 1st January 1991 because the cost of those items is £5,500 each and to purchase them you will need to find a further £1,000 from some other source. In other words, inflation has eroded the value of your money receivable and in real terms, i.e. in terms of what money will buy for you, you have received less for your goods sold than you would have received if you had received the money immediately on sale on 1st January 1990. (Still with us, Chancellor?)

Since inflation is effectively out of your control, i.e. it is a 'macro economic' effect – the result of a national wages/ prices spiralling and more (we've lost the Chancellor now!) – then if you cannot affect it you must take measures to reduce or eliminate the damage it can do to your business. There are two basic ways in which you can deal with this, both depending on your ability reasonably to predict inflation over the short term, i.e. up to a year.

The first measure is to treat the erosion in value of money as a cost of your business and, like any other overhead, include it in your overall costing analysis and therefore effectively reflect the cost in your pricing policy. In other words, you set your prices to allow you to recover the lost value of money as part of your profit. Such a solution has two drawbacks. Firstly – and from your point of view less importantly – it will not go down well with the government of the day since what you are

[ 7 ]

doing is itself inflationary and helping to push up prices in the wages/prices inflationary spiral. Since you might reasonably argue that the government is presiding over a national problem on which you cannot have any influence, and since you might think that the government is causing it anyway, then you may feel little remorse for adding to the government's headaches in this way. (Sorry, Chancellor.) Secondly – and of much more significance to you – your prices may become uncompetitive and you may lose custom by taking this course of action. Over a long term you may be showing greater foresight than your competitors since their failure to do what you are doing may result in their eventual collapse, but as my old economics teacher reminded us all, 'In the long term we are all dead anyway' and your business has to survive in the short term, so this course of action may be a difficult one to pursue.

Another action you can take, and one which may well be more appropriate, is to reduce the effect of inflation by charging interest on your debts. In this way your prices are set at a figure appropriate to the current value of money and if you make a sale which is paid for immediately, then the long-term effects of inflation will have no bearing on your spending power of that money; whereas if you extend credit to your customers and add interest to the debt to take account of inflation, then you are more justly effectively increasing the price of your products only to those who are costing you the loss in value of money. This has the other positive effect of encouraging your debtors to pay more quickly. There are specific points regarding interest on debts and these are covered in another section. (See page 45.)

To go back to our example (shoes and socks off, Chancellor – you'll need every help to counting you can get on this one): if you sell an item for £10,000 on 1st January

[ 8 ]

1990 and you receive the money immediately, then you have the £10,000 to buy the two items you need to purchase of £5,000 each. If you sell the same product on 1st January 1990, still at £10,000, but allow your debtor a year to pay *and* charge him 10% interest, then when you receive the money you receive £11,000 on 1st January 1991 and this £11,000 will enable you to buy the same two items now costing £5,500 each.

All the above suggestions depend for their success on your not underestimating the annual inflation to come (and if you can't do it, Chancellor, I don't know how we're supposed to). In times of uncertain government policy this can be difficult and in the 1960s and early 1970s, when inflation was by any reasonable Western standard 'out of control', many businesses collapsed as they watched the value of their money quickly eroded (and trying to rectify the problem by increasing the prices of subsequent sales only added to the inflation problem).

As an extreme example, in some South American countries inflation has raged at, say, 300% and in those circumstances it demonstrates that a failure to address this problem would very quickly collapse any business. Your £10,000 received one year after sale would be all you had to buy two items now costing £5,000 × 300% each, i.e. they now cost £15,000 *each* – you could not even afford one!

At least you haven't had that problem, Chancellor – yet!

- **Inflation erodes the value of money. Predict it and prepare for it.**

## THE CASHFLOW SYSTEM

'It is only by not paying one's bills that one can hope

to live in the memory of the commercial classes.'
(Oscar Wilde)

Credit is the heart of the cashflow system. Without
credit there would be perfect cashflow: money earned
would be received when earned, and money due to
others would be paid immediately when the goods or
services had been supplied, in other words, as soon as it
became due.

Because of credit – the giving and taking of time to pay
– there is a difference between the time money is earned
or spent and the time when it actually goes into or out of
the business bank account (or Arthur Daley's back
pocket, whichever the case may be).

Cashflow forms the bridge between the accounts and
the bank balance.

Suppose that you buy goods for £500 on the 1st of
August and agree to pay for them on the 1st of September. You sell the goods immediately in August, for £800,
and agree to receive the money for them on the 1st of
October. From the *accounts* point of view you have made
a profit of £300 in the month of August. Don't pat
yourself on the back yet. In terms of *cashflow* you've not
only made nothing, you've made yourself bankrupt. In
September you have to find £500 to pay for the goods you
bought, and subsequently sold, but you haven't any
money and you know that you won't be receiving the
£800 you're owed until October.

Of course, in reality these transactions are part of an
on-going process of many transactions, where proceeds
of earlier sales pay for later purchases, and so on. But this
should not fool you into thinking the example is wrong;
the complexity of the real situation just masks the truth.
And don't underestimate the severity of the problem,
either: as a practising Chartered Accountant with direct

involvement in over 600 small businesses and knowledge of many more, and as a business consultant to many larger companies, I can say from experience that bad cashflow has been the single most common cause of failure in businesses that I have seen collapse. The products are often good, the pricing policy often right – indeed in many cases high demand has proven the basis of the business to be sound – but if the cashflow dries up – if the money to keep the business cycle moving is not there – then disaster follows.

[ 11 ]

To keep trade going, recognising that this problem exists, businesses often turn to the banks to borrow money. We shall look at this in later chapters and it is a perfectly correct course of action. *But* . . . the cost of borrowing is a real cost to the business which eats into the profits, and in times of high interest rates (in other words, when money costs a lot to borrow) businesses that run on a small profit margin quickly find themselves working on a small loss margin, getting bigger!

Opposite is an example of a typical cashflow summary with assumed figures. You will see that there are two columns for each month; *Forecast* and *Actual*. The forecast figures are prepared for the year ahead in total using your best estimates of how the business is going to go; remember that you are accounting for income and payments when they fall due, not when they are 'earned' on paper.

You start from the opening bank balance that is actually in your bank, so the forecast and actual figures at the top left of the sheet will be the same. For predicting the remaining estimates you should consider past trends, how the money came in and went out last year, which will help to predict the effects of 'seasonal' trading. You should also consider the effects of what you reasonably expect to happen this year based on such information as new clients you know you are going to work for or sell to, and future orders already placed.

In predicting expected income from debtors (credit sales) you should realistically consider how your debtors have performed in the past. Repayments, some figures can be predicted accurately, for example rent and rates, and some with a fair degree of accuracy, such as electricity. Others will be more unpredictable. There will be one-off items such as capital expenditure to be considered; this is useful because the forecast may indicate a

## Table 1   Typical cashflow summary

| CASH FLOW FORECAST CHART | Jan. Forecast | Jan. Actual | Feb. Forecast | Feb. Actual | March Forecast | March Actual | April Forecast | April Actual | May Forecast | May Actual | June Forecast | June Actual | July Forecast | July Actual | August Forecast | August Actual | Sept. Forecast | Sept. Actual | Oct. Forecast | Oct. Actual | Nov. Forecast | Nov. Actual | Dec. Forecast | Dec. Actual |
|---|---|---|---|---|---|---|---|---|---|---|---|---|---|---|---|---|---|---|---|---|---|---|---|---|
| Opening Bank Balance b/fwd | 1,000 | 1,000 | 1,580 | | 2,010 | | 1,510 | | 840 | | 1,800 | | 1,620 | | 2,250 | | 990 | | ( 910) | | (1,930) | | (2,950) | |
| Income: | | | | | | | | | | | | | | | | | | | | | | | | |
| from Sales (Cash) | 500 | | 200 | | 300 | | 400 | | 600 | | 200 | | 300 | | 200 | | 300 | | 600 | | 200 | | 400 | |
| from Sales (Debtors) | 2,500 | | 2,600 | | 2,700 | | 1,800 | | 3,900 | | 3,300 | | 2,500 | | 3,700 | | 1,800 | | 1,200 | | 1,300 | | 1,500 | |
| from Interest earned | | | | | 30 | | | | | | 40 | | | | | | 20 | | | | | | 80 | |
| from VAT recoverable | | | | | | | 20 | | | | | | | | 60 | | | | | | | | | |
| from Other Sources (Sundry) | | | | | | | | | | | | | | | | | | | | | 300 | | | |
| Income Sub-Total | 3,000 | | 2,800 | | 3,030 | | 2,220 | | 4,500 | | 3,540 | | 2,800 | | 3,960 | | 2,120 | | 1,800 | | 1,800 | | 1,980 | |
| Expenditure: | | | | | | | | | | | | | | | | | | | | | | | | |
| for Purchases (Cash) | 100 | | 200 | | 50 | | 200 | | 50 | | 600 | | 200 | | 100 | | 300 | | 400 | | 500 | | 100 | |
| for Purchases (on Credit) | 700 | | 600 | | 500 | | 900 | | 800 | | 700 | | 500 | | 600 | | 800 | | 900 | | 1,000 | | 900 | |
| Salaries and Wages (Net) | 200 | | 200 | | 200 | | 200 | | 200 | | 200 | | 200 | | 200 | | 200 | | 200 | | 200 | | 200 | |
| PAYE Payments | 70 | | 70 | | 70 | | 70 | | 70 | | 70 | | 70 | | 70 | | 70 | | 70 | | 70 | | 70 | |
| Rent/Rates | | | | | 1,500 | | | | | | 1,000 | | | | | | 1,500 | | | | | | 1,000 | |
| Light/Heat/Telephone | 300 | | | | | | 400 | | | | | | 150 | | | | | | 200 | | | | | |
| Interest Charges | | | 50 | | 100 | | | | | | 100 | | | | | | 100 | | | | | | 100 | |
| HP/Lease Payments | 50 | | 200 | | 50 | | 50 | | 50 | | 50 | | 50 | | 50 | | 50 | | 50 | | 50 | | 50 | |
| VAT Payments | | | 50 | | | | | | 300 | | | | | | 200 | | | | | | - | | | |
| Advertising/Promotions | | | | | | | 70 | | 70 | | | | | | | | | | | | | | | |
| Capital Expenditure | | | | | | | | | | | | | | | 3,000 | | | | | | | | | |
| Other (Specify) = | | | | | | | | | | | | | | | | | | | | | | | | |
| = | | | | | | | | | | | | | | | | | | | | | | | | |
| Dividend Payments/or Proprietor's Drawings | 1,000 | | 1,000 | | 1,000 | | 1,000 | | 2,000 | | 1,000 | | 1,000 | | 1,000 | | 1,000 | | 1,000 | | 1,000 | | 1,000 | |
| | 2,420 | | 2,370 | | 3,530 | | 2,880 | | 3,540 | | 3,720 | | 2,170 | | 5,220 | | 4,020 | | 2,820 | | 2,820 | | 3,420 | |
| Closing Bank Balance c/fwd | 1,580 | | 2,010 | | 1,510 | | 840 | | 1,800 | | 1,620 | | 2,250 | | 990 | | ( 910) | | (1,930) | | (2,950) | | (4,390) | |

better or worse time to make this purchase; in our example it also produces a VAT refund in that quarter.

In predicting 'proprietor's drawings' – as in our example – you will need to know what personal needs have to be met. If you have known exceptional expenditure to meet, remember to build this into the cashflow forecast, because even though it is not a part of the business your need to draw the extra *will* affect the business. Again, this prediction will allow you to plan the best financial time for the expense, a holiday perhaps.

As the example shows, in September the cashflow becomes negative, in other words you will go overdrawn in the bank. By predicting this, you will be able to take steps to deal with it; you might delay the purchase of the capital expenditure, or delay your holiday. You might go to the bank for an overdraft facility, and they will be impressed if you can predict the situation ahead, they will be unimpressed if you walk in and say 'Could I have an overdraft, as I've already got one!'

You might find you have what is called 'hardcore' overdraft; an overdraft that never clears and never can. To the extent that it reflects the financing of debtors this may be quite acceptable, if it is a progressively increasing trend then it suggests a deeper seated problem; perhaps you are simply not charging enough for your goods, or paying too much interest to finance your debtors. Take steps to deal with this before it is too late! Having done the prediction, then complete the *Actual* columns each month; do it promptly, the value of this information is that it should be made available quickly so that you can do something about it before it gets out of hand. As the situation changes, so modify the forecast columns to take account of your new, more up-to-date, knowledge. And remember, remember that this is not a firework display for your passive entertainment. Don't just watch the

*Actual* column get progressively worse than the *Forecast* and just go 'Oooh!' and 'Aaah!' Do something about it quickly.

The areas that most affect cashflow, that are relevant to this book, are the prompt collection of debts and the reduction of interest charges for financing them. Be aware of this all the time. The cashflow will tell you what the effect of your policies are, and show the true cost to you of them. Act on the information.

- **Cashflow charts are not there to be watched dispassionately. They are to be acted on, and acted on quickly.**

## SALES REPS VERSUS CREDIT CONTROLLERS

'With or backs to the wall, and believing in the justice of our cause, each one of us must fight on to the end.' (Earl Haig)

In a 'one-man' or small 'family' business, most or all of the decisions are taken by one person who, when making a sale on credit, has to take account of the risks involved, which are probably his own risks. The questions one must ask oneself are discussed in other sections of the book.

In slightly larger companies, and even more so in very large companies, the decisions that make sales and the decisions to extend credit will probably be divided between two departments. On the one hand there will be sales reps on the road attempting to sell to customers, and on the other hand there will be an in-house credit control department who have to make the decision whether to extend credit to customers, and to chase debts.

There is an inherent conflict between these two groups and improper control over this conflict can result in the business suffering. It is the owner of the business or the managing director of the Board who has to resolve this conflict constructively in order that the company makes the best balance of decisions between these groups. The MD will need skills such as even hostage-negotiators can only dream of!

The sales reps will see their job, correctly, as making sales; they will see their role as converting potential customers into actual customers, of convincing customers that they require their firm's products and certainly of convincing customers that they require those products as opposed to the products of competitors. Part of their sales 'patter' will be stressing their own firm's ability to deal with the order speedily and efficiently. They will have a tendency to disregard the risks involved in selling on credit, or at least be very relaxed in this respect, and they will be willing to sell to high-risk customers because they will see it as their role to place the sale and that of the credit control departments to concern themselves with such minor trivialities as collecting the money.

The credit control departments are likely to be less than enthusiastic about some of these selling techniques, to about the same degree that whales are less than enthusiastic about whaling ships. This stems partly from the conflict of personalities involved; good salesmen are not book-keepers and generally speaking keep very bad paperwork, and they are almost always prepared to cut corners for the sake of speed, if that means they can make more sales. On the other hand, credit control departments *are* book-keepers and well-run departments will insist on proper documentation in all cases. These two demands are in conflict.

The managing director must resolve this conflict by compromise, pointing out that sales, increasing the sales, and important orders must be made in order that the company succeeds, but that the only sales worth anything at all are those which pay. Therefore the sales reps must be encouraged to make sales bearing in mind the recovery of debts as a criterion. On the other hand, it must also be stressed to the credit control department that they cannot eliminate all risks in assessing whether to extend credit to a customer, nor take excessive time to decide how much credit to extend. They have to take

[ 17 ]

some risk in making the decision quickly in order to obtain the order and not lose it to a competitor.

An influencing factor that the board can use to control over-enthusiastic salesmen is to ensure that they are not paid commission based only on sales orders placed, but that bad debts will somehow affect the sales reps' total commission earned. This must be a compromise as it is not fair to limit the sales reps' commission to monies received because the actual credit control, debt recovery and the risks taken with regard to each customer are not entirely in their control. Nor should they be. A bad credit control department which allows customers to delay paying their debts unreasonably would, if this was reflected in the salesman's commission, probably lose the company its best salesmen and reduce the effectiveness of its sales force. As in so many aspects of corporate decision, making the compromise is a difficult balance of decisions to be made and it is these entre-preneurial skills which demonstrate the real abilities of the managing director or entrepreneur. And if the MD can succeed with all that, then the next United Nations peacekeeping force has found its leader.

- **Risk is part of normal business activity: balancing risk with caution is what makes a successful businessman.**

## THE CAUSES OF BAD DEBTS

'All decent people live beyond their incomes nowa-days, and those who aren't respectable live beyond other people's. A few gifted individuals manage to do both.' ('Saki')

There is no limit to the ingenuity of people in finding

reasons for not paying their debts. But there are very common reasons why businesses collapse and it is worth noting these, not least because many of them are predictable and you can avoid lending to, or extending credit to, businesses likely to end up in these sorry states.

## Overtrading

It seems, at face value, that all businesses should work on the basis of 'the more, the merrier'. In fact, this was only ever true for Robin Hood. A very large number of businesses fail because they take on too much without having the resources to cope with the demand they are trying to meet.

As a simple example of this, where a retail outlet is buying goods for re-sale, it has to fund the stock purchases from its own funds or from what it can borrow. If it finds that the cost of investment in equipment and staff to meet the demand has exhausted the available funds, then it will be unable to afford its purchasing needs. Expansion is, of course, a good thing, but only if it is well planned. The supplier who will be owed money by this company should be wary of constantly increasing orders, particularly if time taken to pay is getting longer and longer, or payment is becoming erratic and unreliable. These are the signs that overtrading may be starting to erode the financial base.

## Lack of working capital

This can follow as a result of overtrading, or it can represent poor management on the part of the proprietors. Working capital is the liquid funds or 'near-liquid' funds available to finance the day-to-day running of the business. If a company exercises poor credit control (i.e. failing to chase its own debtors), then it will not have money to pay its creditors – *you*! It may also be that in small businesses, or 'one man bands', the proprietors are so enthused with their success that they insist on that new Ferrari or weekly holidays to the Bahamas. The business may be basically sound, but if poor management drains away the money then it won't be available to pay your bills. Such management will help the company on its way in the same manner as the iceberg helped the Titanic on *its* way. As a person considering giving credit to companies, watch the Press for information on larger companies, and keep an eye on the proprietors of small businesses. And another eye on their Ferraris.

## Bad stock control

When is stock sold? I have asked this question to many top management trainees on courses I hold and I have

yet to hear the right answer first time. *Stock is never sold!*
You might sell tomorrow the items that are on your shelves today, but you will replace them immediately with
new stock. So there will always be a quantity of stock that
is never sold and money tied up in it is lost for ever. Poor
stock ordering causes many businesses to fail, so open
eyes when you are walking around your customer's
premises could tell you a lot about how much money
they are wasting in this way; as this depletes the money
available to pay bills, it will give you a hint as to what
your chances of recovering your debts are.

Proper stock control is a very complex procedure
designed to reduce the cost of money 'thrown away' in
this manner, but is outside the scope of this book.

### Key man failures
Many businesses, mostly the small ones but sometimes
even very large Public Limited Companies, rely on
certain talented or charismatic individuals to keep the
company going. If they leave, the company often either
collapses quickly or decays slowly. In either case, there
will be some unlucky bad debts along the way, and that
could include your bill. Be wary of companies so clearly
dependent on 'key men'. (Don't avoid them – they can be
the most successful sometimes, or for some of the time.
But be wary.)

### Key suppliers or customers
The old adage warns against never putting all your eggs
in one basket. Businesses learn the truth of this with
great pain. If companies have only one source of supply
for their main 'bread and butter' products, then what
happens if the supplier goes out of business, or decides
that that line is no longer viable for it? Or if a company
has only one key customer for its product and decides to
'shop around'? Try to imagine businesses as lines of

dominoes, with yours in the middle. Then think of those world record attempts to make as many as possible fall over by just knocking one!

## Signs of affluence
When you are looking around your customer's premises, you will be able to see whether or not cashflow is tight by the state of the workplace. Old, damaged furniture, unrepaired broken windows, and a whole host of other signs are suggestive that money is not being made available to the business. At the moment, perhaps the company is still paying it's debts; one day even that may have to be neglected. Consider these impressions when you are deciding whether or not to extend credit.

Be wary of apparently affluent signs also; if the proprietor's office is plush while the rest of the workplace is scruffy, it may mean the proprietor considers himself or herself above the business, and will – when money is tight – rather pay the instalments on their £5,000 leather suite than on your bills. But even overwhelming affluence is to be watched carefully; Sir Kenneth Cork, a leading insolvency specialist, once listed signs of ostentation as signs of impending collapse: a flagpole in the grounds, a Rolls-Royce in the chairman's parking spot, a fountain in reception. Businesses in trouble sometimes try to buy their way out by impressing their customers with their success. If true, all well and good; but if it is just show, then eventually the chickens will come home to roost – in the bankruptcy courts. Where you and your customer will be standing side by side!

As with all business rules, there are no absolutes. Don't avoid people too easily, you will lose good custom. But be cautious, and watch for adverse signs in those who are likely to owe you money. Don't be afraid to 'check out' new customers by making them pay cash first until you feel you can trust them. Don't let them lull you into a false sense of security by gradually increasing their indebtedness to you. And don't lull *yourself* into a false sense of security in your eagerness to make sales; remember that bad debts wipe out huge chunks of profit very quickly!

- **Keep your eyes open at all times.**


## EFFECT ON TRADERS

'I don't owe a penny to a single soul – not counting tradesmen, of course.' (P. G. Wodehouse)

When a debt is irrecoverable it is called 'going bad' and this is the basis of the expression 'bad debts'. There are a host of reasons why debts 'go bad'; but the effect of bad debts can be considerably worse for certain types of businesses than others.

Where suppliers of services, such as the solicitor we considered earlier, do not get paid for their work then they have certain 'hard' losses: the cost of paper used in writing their letters, unrecovered secretarial time, and so on. But their losses are mostly 'soft losses', i.e. the loss of their own time that could have been charged to a client who did pay. So if a bill of £500 is not recovered, the solicitor will have basically to repeat the effort to earn a similar sum; he or she will need to do a further £500 of work (perhaps a little more to recover the costs of the paper, secretary, etc.)

For a trader the 'hard' losses are so much more. Let us say he buys goods for £400 and sells them for £500 (we will ignore the incidental costs of paper and secretary, though the same applies here as to the solicitor). One of his debts, of £500, goes bad. He has lost £500, just like the

solicitor. To recover that £500 will take more than the same effort, it will need *five times* the effort. He will have to sell £2,500 of goods, less his costs of £2,000, to get back the £500 lost. Furthermore, he will have to finance the purchase of the £2,000 of goods for a period, adding to his overheads.

The reason for this is basically simple: profitability. Service industries are highly profitable, as they run no 'costs of sales' expenses. A solicitor's office may return a net profit of 80% of sales. Manufacturing and retail industries, however, may return a net profit of only 8%. To recover the 100% lost when a sale is not paid for requires a lot of eight percents , but very few eighty percents.

It should be recognised that there is a price for the huge profitability in service industries; solicitors can only sell their hours of work to one client at a time whereas the owners of retail businesses, through their many shop outlets and many cash tills per shop, can be selling to hundreds of people at the same time. By spreading the risk so much thinner, recovery for the shop is more certain.

So the next time your solicitor presents you with a whopping great bill for some menial service his clerk did in his sleep, you'll sympathise with the poor old chap, won't you? So make his day and pay him promptly. Or you can really disorient him – give him a tip!

- **Bad debts need to be paid for – by you!**

## WHY BAD DEBTS CAN BE *GOOD* FOR THE BUSINESS

> ' "One can't believe impossible things."
> "I daresay you haven't had much practice", said the Queen.
> "When I was your age, I always did it for half-an-hour a day. Why sometimes I've believed as many as six impossible things before breakfast." ' (Lewis Carroll)

It is difficult to imagine recommending bad debts, i.e. debts which are never recovered, as being good for the business or a healthy sign. However, to a limited degree this is the case.

Excessive bad debts reflect bad management on your

part; they mean that you have wasted a good deal of time, effort and money which you cannot recover, they mean that your cashflow is severely damaged and the amount of capital available for continuation or expansion is restricted. Ultimately, they can mean the collapse of your business. They also mean that you have been irresponsibly relaxed in giving credit to people who cannot be trusted and that you have probably not pursued your debt collection as vigorously as you should have done. There is therefore no excuse for failing to pursue all debts before they become bad and to make every effort to recover sums due to you.

That said, however, the company with no bad debts is also making mistakes. To vet potential customers so vigorously as to eliminate all of those who may become bad debts almost certainly means that you are being overcautious and missing many productive sales opportunities. It means that you are probably not taking sufficient risk in extending credit to some potential customers who would, in fact, be good, paying, customers.

There is a fine balance between precaution and recklessness and one which demands the most fiendish managerial skills of the entrepreneur. However, a successful and growing business must take some chances and a small percentage of bad debts probably suggests that the company is taking sensible risks, but not reckless ones.

In the banking industry, managers who have the power to grant loans are not expected to grant loans to obvious bad risks. On the other hand, the manager who turns in a perfect recovery of all loans made is likely to be criticised for probably having turned away to competing banks some good customers due to an overcautious desire not to suffer bad debts. This is, in fact, true of all businesses where credit is normal.

The proper treatment of the cost of this risk, i.e. the cost of the small percentage of bad debts you will suffer, is to attempt to predict them, broadly speaking on the basis of past experience, and to build into your costing and therefore your pricing policy a recovery of the expected amount.

Credit card companies are the easiest example of where this is openly done, although it must be said that they have come under considerable social and political criticism for being too relaxed in extending credit to those unable to pay for it, knowing that they can simply pass on the cost of certain people's defaults to non-defaulting customers. Social or political implications aside, they are at least dealing with the debt problem positively.

If you can reasonably predict bad debts and account for them in your pricing policy, then there is also a very positive effect on you as the businessman. It means that you do not have to feel negatively about the bad debts, any more than you would have to do about having to pay the electricity or the telephone bills; it means that you do not spend time and energy agonising over every small loss, but free your energies for pursuing more sales. It gives you a healthier outlook towards the business environment in which you are working.

None of this should be taken as an excuse for complacency. You should not allow bad debts to become an unreasonable cost, any more than you should fail to exercise reasonable control over the use of electricity or the telephone in your business, or indeed the control of any costs, but it does put bad debts on a par with these other costs: to be controlled rather than feared. It means that the fear and the negative reaction to bad debts by some businessmen can be eliminated if they recognise that they are dealing with 'just another cost'.

There are obviously specific steps that must be taken to

ensure that bad debts stay at a reasonable level. Many of these are covered in other sections, but in particular it must be stressed that while you may extend a small amount of credit to a customer you believe to be risky, you should never extend an excessive credit. The actual amount we are talking about here will depend on the size of your business and the costs of your individual products, also the frequency of purchases by that customer. If your usual sales to any one customer are £1,000 and your total bad debts in a year are anticipated to be £5,000, then should you be offered an extraordinary deal where you can sell £50,000 to a new customer, you cannot simply think 'Well, this is a risk I should take.' This is a risk that you should mitigate considerably by asking for an advance payment or by payment against a supply in stages.

Getting the balance right is not easy for any business man or woman, but then if it *was* easy we would all be doing it, wouldn't we?

- **Moderation in all things – neither extreme caution nor extreme recklessness will lead to success.**

# SECTION 2

# HOW TO AVOID BAD DEBTS

## CREDIT CHECKS AND REFERENCES

'Prevention is better than cure.' (Proverb)

Before extending credit to any customer, it is sensible to take some form of reference as to reliability as a good payer. Obviously the value involved must be considered here and it is not wise to spend money obtaining checks and references for very small items. In such cases it may be advisable to make an intuitive judgment, extend the credit and see how well the customers perform. If they perform well, then this adds to your confidence in extending further credit at a later date. *However*, be warned that occasionally clever and unscrupulous debtors will use this to lull you into a false sense of security by gradually building up their credit-worthiness and then hitting you with a debt that will feel something like Mike Tyson's boxing glove in full flow. Caution as ever.

For larger debts the first useful source of information is, as above, their own performance on previous debts with you. If a customer is a notorious bad payer, then you hardly need credit references to confirm this, though in fact references may be useful to discover whether they

[ 31 ]

are worse with others, i.e. have judgment debts against them, and so on.

For all significant debtors-to-be, obtain external references from one of the specialist search companies that perform this service. They will, for a fee, provide you with a report which will list any court judgments given against the potential customer, and any other more serious insolvency information. It may also provide you with information of other financial commitments, which would give some idea of ability to pay and provide you with information on which to make your own judgment.

Other such reports might provide information on a historical basis regarding the profitability of the company or business and its working capital availability, which is the basis of your customer being able to 'pay their way' and therefore pay your invoices.

Be aware that all such information is of necessity out of date and the degree to which it is so could be important. Therefore using your own knowledge of the company is still vital and these references should be regarded as additional rather than alternative information. Considering filing of company accounts, it is highly likely that a company in trouble will delay filing its accounts as long as possible, partly because it is probably not operating efficiently, and not least for the precise reason of suppressing such information from reference reports.

You could also ask potential customers for names of other suppliers to whom you could write for references of their credit-worthiness, though such information must be tempered with the knowledge that these references will have been selected by the customers and therefore ought to show them in the best possible light. If the light is dim from these references, just imagine what a black-out the rest would probably be!

A useful approach to credit checks via your customers' other suppliers is to telephone them. While writing to them produces very useful information for your files and should be undertaken, telephoning them often reveals information that people would be reluctant to put in writing. The approach here is important: if you ask 'Do they pay on time?' you might well be told they do, but if you ask 'I suppose they have trouble paying their bills like the rest of us?', you may well find a sympathetic out-pouring of much more useful information!

- **You wouldn't lend money to some stranger off the street, would you? Well, in fact, that is precisely what you are going to do – get at least some comfort from others who already have.**

## THE USE OF CREDIT LIMITS

'Facts do not cease to exist because they are ignored.' (Aldous Huxley)

In order to avoid being 'conned' into a false sense of security and so extending more and more debt to a customer without deliberate thought, decide on a credit limit and stick to it, not extending more than that amount of credit to a customer at any given time. This does not have to be inflexible, and you can increase their credit limit according to your belief in their trustworthiness, but in this case it will again be a deliberate decision and one you will be forced to *make* rather than one you drift into.

In order to set an appropriate credit limit, you should maintain a record of all information relating to your customer's past payment history, together with any external references from other suppliers, external credit reports from specialist companies and any other information.

It is obviously necessary that anybody involved in making sales, and everybody in your credit control department, is aware of the up-to-date position on the credit limits. It may also be appropriate to have a specific review date when somebody has to make a deliberate decision even to maintain the limit, particularly for customers where there is some doubt. Where appropriate, credit limits can go down as well as up.

Remember that you are not obliged to give credit to anyone, even if it is customary in your business to give credit or even if you yourself are accustomed to giving credit. Furthermore, you do not have to give an explanation to any individual as to why you are not giving them credit. They may try to bluff you by suggesting that to breach 'custom and practice' is a form of defamation of their character; this is garbage. You don't owe anybody a living, even at attractive rates of interest.

On the basis that a bird in the hand is worth two in the bush, it is obviously preferable not to give credit if you can obtain cash instead. Where possible, do as Woody Allen said: 'Take the money and run.' Therefore the simple rule on credit is that you should only give it when you have to, for as little time as necessary and you should vigorously pursue recovery as soon as possible. Do not consider credit to be something you ought to give; if your competition is not giving credit, then there is no reason for you to do so. Even the successful recovery of debts is no substitute for not having them in the first place.

- **Giving credit is always a deliberate decision. Let it be so on your part rather than that of your customer.**

## MINIMUM CREDIT ORDERS

'Small is beautiful.' (E. F. Schumacher)

There are basically two reasons why you should impose a minimum value on sales against which you are prepared to extend credit.

Firstly, there is the question of your own administration costs in putting an amount through the debtor's ledger procedures and the administration costs of collecting a debt. Even though your customer may appreciate it and even if it is paid on time, you may have made no profit at all by the time you cost out the hours of manpower needed to record this more complex (than cash) transaction. There is no way to put a general value on this figure as it will vary from business to business, but your internal costing procedures should enable you to calculate some figure below which only cash with order or cash on delivery is economically acceptable.

Secondly, you must be honest (or cynical, depending on your point of view) and recognise that there is a minimum figure against which you cannot pursue a potentially bad debt. If you are owed a very small amount, then it will never be economical to pursue the debtor to the end, i.e. to the courts, or to employ even basic debt collection procedures such as targeted letters and telephone calls. Not only will you know this from the outset but so will your debtor and any threat you make against a very small sum will sound hollow, because the debtor will know that you are unlikely to carry it through. You could, of course, make it a point of principle to pursue all debts and let it be known that you do, but this is unlikely to be productive; it will show that you are not thinking through your forward planning of the business very efficiently and this will not gain you the admiration of your customers. It will probably result

in some 'badwill' which could otherwise have been avoided and it will certainly result in some frustration on your part.

Find out what the minimum figure is relative to this kind of consideration and do not extend credit where it is uneconomical to process or recover it. You can even make it very clear to would-be debtors that this is the reason you are restricting the giving of credit and by and large they will respect your business judgment.

Only one good reason exists for breaking the two above rules: to extend credit to a potentially more valuable customer in the hope of gaining their goodwill. It is also a good way of testing the degree to which they keep to agreed credit terms, but unless you feel that your efforts can turn into a mighty oak then it is probably not worthwhile doing it. Nobody needs a pocket full of acorns.

- **Debtors cost time and money. When they cost more time and money than the value of the debt, they are not worth having.**

## CREDIT INSURANCE

'You cannot be insured for the accidents that are most likely to happen to you.' (Alan Coren)

It is possible to insure your debts against non-recovery; but it is an expensive form of insurance because of the distinct probability that it may have to pay out! Except in special circumstances, it is probably more cost than you are likely to risk, particularly if you have a wide spread of debts (and most will not default). Insurance companies will also examine your debtors and only offer to cover, at least at realistic rates, potentially good debts; they will not want to deal with potential bad debts, which pretty well explains the success of insurance companies!

Even if you do insure a debt and it fails, the procedure for claiming and settlement is often so drawn out that many harmful effects of the bad debt have happened anyway, before you receive your money.

- **Insurance is a very exceptional item for very particular circumstances only.**

## INVOICES

> 'In architecture as in all other operative Arts, the end
> must direct the Operation. The end is to build well.
> Well building hath three conditions: Commodity,
> Firmness, and Delight.' (Henry Wotton.)

As any management consultant will say, with tongue
only slightly in cheek, the object of enterprise is to transfer money from your customer's bank account to your
bank account with the minimum of fuss. Once the goods
have been sold or the services provided, then it is the
invoice, i.e. the demand for payment, that is the means
to this painless transfer.

It can be painful if simple, basic rules about the design
of the invoice are ignored.

Another rule of business is that people are, depending
on your point of view, either extremely lazy or extremely
overworked; whichever they are, they will do what is
made easy for them before they will do what is difficult.

Combining these two rules therefore, it is obvious that
a well designed invoice is likely to result in getting paid
all the more promptly.

### Design of the invoice format

Your invoices, whether they are preprinted, a template
on the computer or handwritten from a duplicate book,
should contain the following basic data:

1. The full name and address of the company and the
   name of the proprietor or another appropriate
   person who can be contacted with queries on the
   invoice.
2. The accounts department address, or the address to
   which the remittance should be paid, if different
   from 1. In this case you must make very clear and
   prominent which address the cheque is to be sent to.

3.  The full telephone number of your company. Do not simply put 'Anytown 1234', but also give the national dialling code for Anytown so your customer does not need to look it up in the dialling code book – just a small inconvenience of this kind might be sufficient for them to throw the item into their in-tray rather than deal with it immediately.
4.  Your VAT number.
5.  A prominent invoice number which can always be used as the basis of correspondence or communication about the invoice. In preprinted invoices these may be sequentially numbered or you may keep an invoice day book cross-referencing each invoice issued to the book, so that the proper sequence can be maintained.
6.  If you are proposing to charge interest on overdue payments, then this must be specifically stated on the invoice including the terms of interest, the rate of interest and the date from which interest will run. (See the section in this book on interest charging on page 45.)

**Specific invoices**

Having designed a basic invoice template, draw up each individual invoice with equal precision. Each invoice should contain the following:

1.  The tax point and date of invoice. These are usually one and the same.
2.  Clear and precise details of what the invoice is raised in respect of, including details of delivery dates, order numbers or order references. The object of this is that your customer should not be in any doubt as to what they are being asked to pay for and should be able to cross-reference your invoice to their own

documentation. Use their own references as much as possible.

3.  The invoice should contain a due date by which it is payable. It is not a good idea to use terms such as 'thirty days' as one of the favoured excuses of the slow payer is 'Oh, I miscounted and didn't realise it was due yet'. Alternatively, you might be offered the excuse 'We thought it meant thirty days from the end of the month', and so on. Put the date due on the invoice: 'Invoice to be settled by the 8th February 199–'. Specifying the date on which it is due makes it very clear to the customer when to make the payment and also adds to the psychological pressure on them to meet a specifically imposed deadline.

4.  The calculation of VAT and the amount of VAT applicable. They may well have to process this into their own paperwork and if they have to take the trouble to extract the VAT from a gross figure (a relatively complex calculation of dividing by twenty-three and multiplying by three in the case of 15% VAT) then again they are likely to throw this into the in-tray until an indefinite later date rather than deal with it immediately. This will be particularly true where the customer is a 'one man band' but also applies where large companies employ sometimes less than enthusiastic purchases control staff. If you can free them from the drudgery of work so they have time to check out the form of their next bet at Doncaster, or polish their nails, you will be doing both of you a great service.

**General**
There are a few other techniques which may make your invoices more 'user friendly' and likely to speed up the payment:

1. Your customer will have to keep the invoice in their own records as proof of purchase and payment and cannot therefore return it to you together with their cheque. However, they will not want to have to draw up a letter to enclose with the cheque explaining why they are paying you. It is therefore a very good idea to provide a 'two set' invoice, one of which is the invoice proper and one of which is the remittance advice to be returned together with the cheque. This then enables the customer to simply attach their cheque to the remittance advice, put it in an envelope and post it with the minimum of difficulty on their part. Alternatively, design an invoice with a 'tear-off' remittance advice attached.

2. It is advisable to make invoices A4 size since that is by far the most popular size of paper used commercially and therefore anything smaller would simply get lost in the piles of paperwork in the customer's in-tray. If you attach a tear-off remittance advice, it is advisable to add this to the right-hand side of the A4 sheet which then 'flags out' your invoice whenever it is put amongst other A4 sheets.

3. Your invoice will have to reflect to some degree your 'house colours', but to the extent that it can be done it is advisable to make your invoice brightly coloured – this will also help to keep bringing attention to it if it is lying on a person's desk. One client I knew made his invoices a revolting, fluorescent pink so that customers would pay up just to be rid of them; he swore it worked wonders!

One further point to consider is that efficiency will command respect: you should send out your invoices at the appropriate time because this will show efficiency on the part of your company. They will arrive at your customer's desk while the knowledge of the order is still fresh in their mind and will further add to the pressure on them to respond efficiently and pay you quickly. If you send out your invoice six months after supply of goods then you can hardly complain if you are paid six months after receipt of invoice, not least because your customer will probably (rightly) realise that you are so inefficient it will take you that long to discover what they are up to!

- **A day spent designing your invoice and invoicing procedure could save weeks of effort later.**

## STATEMENTS

'Cry "Havoc!" and let slip the dogs of war.' (William Shakespeare)

Many customers will pay on invoice and there will be no need to issue statements. Generally speaking, statements should only be issued to remind customers of outstanding amounts; this keeps paperwork and costs for you to a minimum. If you have a customer who you know is a habitual slow payer, it does not hurt to send a statement even before payment is due as a second reminder prior to the date to encourage payment at the appropriate time. If your particular business needs it, or if the majority of your customers demand it, then make statements a regular, planned feature of the credit control routine. The only rule is, never issue them without thought.

To be effective, statements must be as well thought out as invoices. Like invoices, they must contain the same basic template information and particularly the appropriate address, the full telephone number and a contact name, since they are more likely to be used during disputes than invoices.

For the particular customer information, each individual invoice should be listed including the date, the invoice number and the full amount due. Do not simply bring forward the balance on the previous statement as this will encourage disputes when slow paying customers argue that they need information about the breakdown of outstanding balances brought forward so that they can check them against their own payments. Ensure that each statement contains all the information needed.

Although it is important that the credit controllers of your company maintain an aged debtors analysis in order to know the age of bad debts and who is causing delayed payments, (see pages 48–50) do not show the aged debtors analysis on the statements (although this is frequently done). It has the implied effect of granting 'approval' to old debts, on the basis that if you have set up a system to account for it it must be acceptable to you. It encourages people to pay more slowly and should be avoided.

Statements can become too 'acceptable' and normal and it does not hurt to write specifically addressed letters in respect of persistent outstanding amounts; these can have the effect of highlighting more easily the outstanding amounts.

The use of 'overdue' stickers can be effective; these can be purchased at any main office supplies shop and are a cheap and effective way of highlighting overdue amounts.

Your invoice and statements procedures should be geared towards your type of business and your type of customer; in some cases, where there are many small

items involved, you can add a statement to the bottom of each invoice, keeping your customer up-to-date with outstanding amounts and keeping up the pressure for payment. On the other hand, where you are dealing with major customers, it is advisable to learn the procedures which best suit their purchase payments department so that your invoices, statements and reminders arrive at the appropriate time for payment and thus avoid the increasingly frequent excuse, 'We only pay out

[ 44 ]

once a month on a cheque run and unfortunately you missed it by one day. . . .'

- **Good statements get good results. Bad statements get bad results.**

## CHARGING INTEREST TO DEBTORS

'Give them the cold steel, boys!' (General Lewis Arminstead)

To reduce the damaging effect of inflation of credit periods extended to your debtors, you may decide to charge interest on delayed payments. This is normal business practice and quite legal, but there are certain rules relating to this.

Firstly, you must consider the business environment in which you are competing and if it is normal to extend an interest free credit period of, say, 30 days or 90 days, or whatever, then you must be prepared to do this also, or risk losing custom to your competitors. In this instance, you must treat the effects of inflation (discussed on pages 6–9) as a cost to be built into your pricing policy. For those debtors who exceed the stated credit periods, or who seek special terms for a special order, consider charging interest for delayed payment.

It is only legally enforceable if you make this term clear in your contract at the time of sale. It may seem like a good idea to charge your customer interest on late payments as an afterthought when the debt is already old, but in this circumstance it will not be legally enforceable as you have not made it a part of the contract at the time the contract was made. (There has been strong lobbying of the government to introduce a statutory right to charge interest on debts which may make such

[ 45 ]

afterthoughts legal, but this is not the case at the time of writing).

The advantage to you of agreeing a late payment interest charge at the time of sale is that any debtors taking an unreasonable time to pay your debts are at least paying for the privilege themselves rather than getting you to pay for it on their behalf – at the cost of your own business.

In the case of very large debts, and where the customer eventually does pay the basic price of the goods but fails to pay the interest charge, then it will be worth your while pursuing the outstanding amount of interest due, but it must be said that in the case of very small amounts, where the interest that is withheld is only a few pounds, it may not be very practical or cost-effective for you to pursue the sums. The real advantage of threatening your debtors with this sum is that it will encourage them to pay you more quickly. It may even be that if they are short of money, they will pay you and not one of your competitors. No crocodile tears here, please, if it is to the detriment of your competitors – 'all's fair in love and war' and getting paid is a battle! It also gives you some leverage in negotiating for the recovery of debts where you can offer to waive an agreed interest for settlement as part of a negotiation, a negotiating tool you would otherwise not have.

As in pressing for any recovery of monies due, you will have to take account of any damage to goodwill that this causes between yourself and your customers and, practically speaking, the success of this policy will depend on your 'clout' in the market.

If it is your policy to charge interest on late payments, then this must be clearly stated on all documentation relating to the sale of the goods or services and in any contract of sales drawn up. It should be stated on invoices and statements, in the terms and conditions of sale and debtors should be reminded of the interest charge in any letters pursuing debts.

- **Someone has to pay for extended credit periods. Don't let it be you.**

## THE USE OF COMPUTERS

> 'One machine can do the work of fifty ordinary men. No machine can do the work of one extraordinary man.' (Elbert Hubbard)

Thanks to the introduction of the personal computer, the proliferation of word processors and the introduction of small computers into even the earliest school classes, computing is no longer the mystery and almost pseudo-religion that it used to be.

Let us be quite clear what computers are *not*. They are not Hal of Arthur C. Clarke's *2001 – A Space Odyssey*. They do not think, they do not resolve problems for us, they do not offer advice and you cannot extract anything from them that you haven't put in in the first place. And they are extremely unlikely to hatch a plot to kill you when you are next floating outside your spacecraft!

As to what computers *are*; related to accounts and credit control, they are super adding machines with an ability to sort information in a variety of ways according to instructions implanted in the software and they have enormous memories capable of storing and retrieving vast quantities of data. They are also incredibly fast and enable data to be collated and made available for use very much quicker than manual systems.

The proper use of a computer system will enable you to be more up-to-date in your knowledge of who owes

[ 47 ]

you money and for how long they have owed it, and will enable you to take more prompt action on those who are not paying you. In addition, it may provide for the quicker and more efficient production of invoices and statements which will themselves aid in receiving payments against debts.

Use your computer wisely. And make it a regular part of your monthly routines to use the output. In the case of credit control, ensure that you have a monthly aged debtors listing, rank in order of importance the debts you are going to chase up and do it!

When I was auditing a large building company some years ago, I was chasing the audit trail of output from the computer; I arrived at one department where the systems analysis indicated a particular output was being sent, and asked the staff there what they did with the print-out of some five hundred pages they were receiving on a monthly basis. 'We put it in that cupboard over there,' they said. Patiently, I rephrased my question. 'What *use* do you make of it in this department?' I asked. 'None,' they said 'we just put it in that cupboard over there.'

- **Garbage in, garbage out. Think of what you want from your computer, design it, and use it.**

## THE AGED DEBTOR SUMMARY

'What do the ravages of time not injure?' (Horace)

It is important for effective control over debtors that your company is aware of how long debts are outstanding, which specific debts are outstanding and which specific customers are slow paying. You must therefore keep an aged debtor summary on a monthly basis in order to provide this information and allow for effective and quick

## Table 2 Example of aged debtor summary

REPORT .............................................

DATE .............................................

AGED DEBTOR SUMMARY   (CREDIT PERIOD ALLOWED 30 DAYS)

PART ONE

| Customer name or reference | Total amount due | Invoices not yet due for payment | Outstanding 30–60 days | Outstanding 60–90 days | Outstanding 90–120 days | Outstanding over 120 days |
|---|---|---|---|---|---|---|
| Customer 1 | £8,000 | £2,200 | £5,000 | | | £ 800 |
| Customer 2 | £2,000 | £2,000 | | | | |
| Customer 3 | £1,500 | | £1,500 | | | |
| Customer 4 | £3,500 | £ 500 | | £2,000 | £1,000 | |
| | £15,000 | £4,700 | £6,500 | £2,000 | £1,000 | £ 800 |

PART TWO   (TARGET 30 DAYS CREDIT PERIOD)

| | |
|---|---|
| Debt outstanding | £10,300 |
| Annual Sales | £108,000 |
| Averaging Debt outstanding: | $\dfrac{£10,300}{£108,000} \times 365 = 34.81 \text{ days}$ |

*Note*:   Debtor period is in adverse variance; explanation to be with Managing Director first thing Monday morning following report date

follow-up by you or your credit control department.

An example of the aged debtor summary is shown above. Its main features are that it clearly shows those invoices which were raised within the payment period (and are therefore not yet due) and then, on a monthly basis, the specific amounts overdue for each month for each individual customer.

For analysis by customer, this then highlights bad payers. It also enables the average debt outstanding to be calculated. The credit control department should be given a target figure and they should be made to explain adverse variances from this. In the case of a one-man company, the average debt should not be allowed to deteriorate past a given standard.

The average debt outstanding is the calculation of the length of time – on average – that you are waiting for payment. Say, for example, that you make sales of £120,000 over a twelve month period, an average of £10,000 per month. If your debtors are £15,000, then the calculation of average debt outstanding is:

$$\frac{£\ 15,000}{£120,000} \times 365 \text{ (days)} = 45.62 \text{ days}$$

This means that on average your debts are remaining due for a period of 45.62 days or – to put it another way – approximately one and a half month's earnings are always owed to you.

You should set a target figure, perhaps 30 days, and work to attain, and maintain, it. This calculation should be done regularly and any lengthening of the period should be controlled, and reduced.

- **The longer the average debt outstanding, the more you are financing your customers by paying interest in your bank for their borrowings.**

## CHEQUES AND SIMILAR FORMS OF PAYMENT

'Though I am not naturally honest, I am so sometimes by chance.' (William Shakespeare)

Even though you may breathe a sigh of relief when you have managed to squeeze a cheque out of your debtor, the story may not be ended. If there are insufficient funds in your debtor's bank account, they will refuse to honour the cheque and it will 'bounce'. Some companies are prone to issuing enough bouncing cheques to defoliate a Malaysian rubber plantation and obviously bad experience should result in caution against accepting cheques from known bouncers. Of course, the vast majority of debt settlement is by cheque and so it might

be advisable to remind your customer that the Theft Act of 1968 makes it a criminal offence to issue a cheque when you know you do not have funds to cover its value. (Don't bother to remind the customer that it is incredibly difficult to prove that a cheque was issued 'knowing' that funds were insufficient.) Follow up all bounced cheques immediately with very strong letters and attempt to recover in cash, if possible, or by a form of guaranteed cheque (see below). Should you receive back a cheque from the bank marked 'refer to drawer', then be sure to keep the cheque. Do not return it to your customer as it may be needed to prove your case in court, particularly if you charge him under the Theft Act.

## Guaranteed cheques

Far better than 'common or garden' cheques are the exotic variety known either as bank certified cheques or bank drafts, both of which are guaranteed.

The bank certified cheque is your customer's ordinary cheque, but pre-certified by the bank so that it must clear and will be honoured.

A bank draft is a cheque issued by the bank on its own account and is absolutely safe (the bank will have already had the funds off your debtor anyway).

It is not practical to ask for guaranteed cheques for each and every normal business transaction as they cost a lot in bank charges to issue, but they are worth asking for in certain circumstances:

1.  Where you have received a bounced cheque and you want something guaranteed rather than another bounced cheque.
2.  Where you are dealing with a particularly large order, perhaps to a new customer or to a customer not usually making such large demands.
3.  Where there is some urgency and you cannot await normal bank clearance time in order to verify that you have received your money properly.

## Promissory notes

A promissory note is a special form of post-dated cheque. It is drawn up by your debtor with his bank and it amounts to a promise to pay on a given date some time in the future. It is far better than a post-dated cheque for a number of reasons. Firstly, it is a written enforceable document which, in the event of being dishonoured, would then be documentary support for your case in a court claim. Secondly, it is an agreement to pay a specific amount on a specific date which is known to the debtor's bank and thus more likely to be honoured, rather than lose face with the bank, whereas post-dated cheques are certainly not drawn up with the bank's knowledge. Thirdly, promissory notes are negotiable, which means that you, having received a promissory note from your debtor, can sell it to somebody else, usually at a discount, in order to obtain your money at an earlier date than that promised (less the discount). Indeed, the City institutions make a business of buying promissory notes, but obviously they will make the appropriate checks to ensure that they are likely to be honoured. Being negotiable, they can also be used as security for loans and other borrowings.

**Bills of Exchange**
A Bill of Exchange is similar to a promissory note but is made out by you and signed for by your debtor accepting its terms.

Both of these last two methods of payment are usually guaranteed by a third party and if the third party is of substance, then you have a much better chance of collecting on the due date. Most often they are backed by guarantees from the banks themselves which make them very secure. Like guaranteed cheques, these are usually only used for exceptional, and not everyday, transactions, though the requirements of certain businesses mean that in particular cases they are more commonly used. They obviously suffer from the disadvantage of being more expensive to arrange than a simple cheque and therefore they do not replace normal cheque transactions.

For those selling overseas, the problems of debt collection are no different, although distance and language barriers can make it more difficult. For debt settlement, however, there are many forms of special payment specific to the exporting industry; those with a yen for dollars and deutschmarks should also consult the export trade bodies.

- **There are guaranteed forms of payment available; if you are suffering from bounced cheques you should insist on these, and if refused offer only cash terms.**

## BANKER'S ORDERS

'A pleasant old buffer, nephew to a lord,
Who believed that the bank was mightier than the sword.' (William Plomer)

Banker's orders are instructions from the account holder to pay certain amounts regularly, or to accept demands from others according to a pre-arranged contract. There are two basic form of banker's order: standing orders and direct debits.

### Standing orders

You instruct your bank to pay a certain amount on a certain date regularly (monthly, annually, etc.) either indefinitely or for a fixed period of time. It is for a specific amount and any variation can only be made by the issue of a new standing order.

### Direct debits

Direct debits do not specify amounts, but merely the person to whom the debit is payable, and so where variable amounts or variations are involved, these are more practical.

Obviously, these forms of payment are most useful

where regular payments or regular periods of payments are involved, e.g. if you are charging someone a monthly rental for office space. It means that the bank, rather than your debtor, is responsible in the first instance for the machinery of paying your debt, but it is no security or guarantee of debt collection, because if your debtor has not got the money in the bank then the bank will refuse to pay the amount due.

Proper arrangement of banker's orders with your customer also means that you may be able to arrange to receive the money quicker than you would do if you had to wait for a normal credit period to expire.

It is often very difficult to get customers to accept these types of banker's order once you are actually doing business with them, and if you intend to use them it may be best to insist on them with your customer from the outset. Indeed, the use of standing orders or direct debits is likely to be dependent on your type of business, in which case either it will be normal for you to use them or you will not use them at all.

(The main advantage of banker's orders is not so much in the field of debt collection, as in the field of marketing. If you are selling a monthly service, such as a monthly magazine or an annual membership subscription or a subscription to a monthly financial report service, then they are useful because they put inertia on your side. Asking people to pay their renewal subscriptions each period will always result in a number failing to do so because they have tired of the service, or even possibly because of their own laziness. The banker's order means that renewal is automatic, unless specific action is taken to cancel it, and in such businesses you will tend to find that you will keep more of your customers for longer, unless you go out of your way to upset them.)

Even their limited use in debt control, however, is not

to be underestimated and, where practical, this should be considered.

- **If you are going to use banker's orders, use them from the outset.**

## CREDIT CARDS

> 'I am sorry I have not learned to play at cards. It is very useful in life.' (Samuel Johnson)

Very often your customers will want credit, but it will not suit you or be possible for you to extend it to them. In certain businesses, a simple solution to this is to apply to the major credit card companies for the right to accept their cards in your business. The credit card companies will then supply you with the necessary equipment to enable you to accept the credit card, when offered. This can be anything from a roller printing machine which embosses the credit card details onto a voucher, then signed by the customer, up to an 'online terminal' which enables you to obtain instant authorisation of credit cards offered by transmitting their details back to the credit card company as the sale is taking place.

The advantage of this solution is that you do not have to extend credit to customers and take risks in their not being credit-worthy. There are disadvantages; in particular, the credit card companies will charge you a percentage, approximately 4%, of the sale, as a fee for the service and this could constitute a substantial reduction in your profitability.

It must also be said that credit card fraud is considerably on the increase and the credit card companies are now, more than ever, challenging retailers who fail to take all the necessary precautions, such as checking lists

of stolen or wanted credit cards and checking signatures.
However, they may be becoming a little 'over-zealous'. I have seen one complaint where a company refused to make payment to the retailer on the basis that the signature was not as on the card (which was in fact a stolen card), but I have to admit that I could see no significant variation and would probably have accepted the signature myself. There is very little the retailer can practically do in this circumstance. (I have yet to manage to get my own signature to look like the one on my credit

card – a three by quarter inch strip just isn't the shape of my signature!)

It is possible that the signature check on credit cards is something which credit card companies will review very soon, as clearly this is a ludicrously flawed part of the system, but until this is done the retailer should beware of credit card companies becoming increasingly stringent in their own enforcements.

There has always been a rule that companies could not differentiate between the price charged for goods paid for in cash and that paid by credit cards. However, suggestions have been made by the government recently, in an effort to dampen the credit boom, to make this differentiation legal and it may soon be possible for your customers to negotiate slightly better rates for themselves by offering you cash or particular credit cards. This would be to your advantage. One hotel I know of already displays an order of preference of the cards that they are prepared to receive, based on the cost to them of accepting the individual types of cards. At present, they cannot pass this difference on to the customer and therefore compliance with it is a matter of goodwill, but once this difference in cost can be passed on, then no doubt there will be a certain amount of change resulting from this competitiveness.

- **Credit cards offer a balance between safer credit and a fairly costly commission. Consider this for your business.**

## DISCOUNTS – THE PROS AND CONS

'Ah, take the Cash in hand and waive the rest.' (Edward Fitzgerald)

In order to give your customers an incentive to pay you,

consider offering them a discount, but this is not to be used as a replacement for good credit control, which should always be as effective as possible.

Discounts should only be offered where they can be enforced. In other words, if you say that you will accept a 2% discount on the amounts due providing the sum is paid within 15 days, then you will have to be absolutely certain that you can enforce this and that your customer will not take two months to pay you and then still claim the discount. In the latter case, you would simply be opening the door to reducing your profits even more and achieving very little. And it is a door your customer will be delighted to walk through time and time again. Should a customer abuse such a system, then it can always be withdrawn, but of course by this time some damage is already done.

Discounts are often expensive, can lead to unpleasant argument and can cause all sorts of problems in even well kept book-keeping systems and control ledgers.

What may be more practical than such a discount system is the system of retrospective discounting. To use this, you would agree with your customer a certain discount which is repayable by you to him (rather than deducted by him at source) based on his *actual* perform-ance rather than promised performance. At the end of each period (i.e. month, quarter, half year or year) you would review their settlement of your debts and if they have complied with the terms of your agreement, then you would make them the appropriate payment in respect of their discount. This then puts the onus on them rather than you.

- **Discounts are expensive and hard to enforce properly. Retrospective discounting is more advisable.**

## FACTORING

> 'What's a thousand dollars? Mere chicken feed. A poultry matter.' (Groucho Marx)

If you are feeling that your cashflow is punitive, one way of financing your debtors rather than going to the bank for a loan or overdraft facility is to factor your debts. The factoring company will approve the various accounts that you offer them and you will then be able to send your invoices to them and they will pay them very much quicker than your debtor. They will also undertake recovery of the debt. They will charge a fee based on a percentage of the debts they are factoring.

It is not a way of avoiding bad debts, as the factoring company's contract will provide for repayment by you of any debts not recovered.

There are some problems with factoring. It is generally an expensive form of correcting cashflow and you should consider other less expensive forms, such as overdraft or bank facilities, to tide you through, particularly if cash flow is stretched only in the short term. You may also find that your customers will view factoring with suspicion as it is held that companies who factor their debts are in financial difficulty and may therefore lose the confidence of some of their customers. Possibly this is an unfair appraisal on their part, but it is nonetheless a widely held opinion. It must be said that there is also support for the argument, since factoring *is* expensive and therefore likely to be one of the last resorts a company turns to, suggesting financial difficulties identified or looming.

Factoring has the advantage from your point of view not only of accelerating the receipt of your debts, but of relieving you of the burden of debt chasing; this is done by the factoring company, who will be more expert at it than you are.

- **Factoring can save you overdraft costs and debt chasing time, but it could cost in prestige as well as money.**

## GUARANTEES

'No one can guarantee success in war.' (Winston Churchill)

If you believe that a person to whom you are considering extending credit may not be sufficiently credit-worthy, and assuming that you still want to extend credit, then you can ask them to obtain a guarantor for the debt. In this instance a third party, the guarantor, would sign a legally drawn up contract agreeing to settle the liability if your debtor, i.e. the person being guaranteed, does not pay.

This obviously increases your chances of eventual recovery, but clearly you must ensure that the guarantor has assets to support the guarantee, or you will simply have doubled the amount of worthless debtors involved and two times nothing is still nothing.

If it is a company which signs a guarantee for another party, then be aware that that company has pledged all its assets in support of that guarantee. (It's worth making sure that all its assets don't also add up to nothing.) Directors of limited liability companies are not personally liable for the company's guarantees.

(Nor indeed are they liable for the company's own debts, unless you have obtained a guarantee from them in respect of these. Small companies requesting overdraft or loan facilities from banks are often given them only if their directors are prepared personally to guarantee the loans, usually by 'putting up' their own houses as security.)

[ 61 ]

Unincorporated businesses, i.e. sole traders and part-
nerships, are personally liable for the debts of their business, but if they are 'men of straw', i.e. they have no real
assets of their own, then a guarantee from a third party
may be advisable. In these cases make sure that you are
aware of the true position. Even though the sole trader
may live in a very large house, it is no good assuming
that when you come to call in your debts you will be able
to claim against it. The trader may have put it in somebody else's name and be personally devoid of assets.
(The amount of builders I know who live in other
people's houses is amazing!) To prevent misunderstand-

ing, make all guarantees legally drawn up documents, and ensure that your solicitor has made the necessary checks to prove that there is substance behind the guarantee.

- **All guarantees must be in writing, and must be backed by worth.**


## AGENCY

'We're overpaying him, but he's worth it.' (Samuel Goldwyn)

Although agency law is very specific, this is often an area of great confusion, particularly to small businesses. Other than 007, an agent is a person acting on your behalf and empowered to do certain things which commit you personally. He (or she) may negotiate contracts on your behalf and is 'Licensed to bill.'

Nobody can make a contract which commits you unless you have given an authority for them to do so. Even then the contract will have to be one of a nature that it would be normal for the agent to make on your behalf and normal for others to expect could be made on your behalf. Once you have informed people that you have an agent working on your behalf, then if you want to terminate this, you must give specific notice to those involved that you have terminated the agency, otherwise you could be held liable for contracts placed after a time when you believed they could not be made.

The law of agency states that a contract made by an agent is binding on the principal who is liable for its terms. If not, then the agent is liable for a breach of specified authority, in which case the principal is not liable.

[ 63 ]

From your point of view, as a supplier to a person who owes you money, there could well be dispute if you have made a contract with somebody's agent and the principal denies that you should have accepted the contract. Agency law provides that you will always have somebody to take to court, i.e. either the principal or the agent. But even if judgment is found in your favour, it does not guarantee that you will recover your money, as it is almost certain that you will not have done any credit

[ 64 ]

or credit-worthiness checks on the agent, believing yourself to be acting with the principal. You may therefore find yourself with judgment against a 'man of straw' – an expression to describe a person with no assets. (It always reminds me of the scarecrow in *The Wizard of Oz*, but then how much money did he ever carry on him?)

Unfortunately, disputes between three parties as to who is liable and whether or not you had any grounds for accepting the contract, or knowing that you should not have done, are complicated and mean that some of these claims can be very long and protracted and recovery, even when successful, can take a great deal of time.

- **Make sure everyone concerned knows who is empowered to act for you. Be sure you understand who acts for others.**


## CONTRA COLLECTIONS

'Fair exchange is no robbery.' (Proverb)

There will be occasions when you will be buying from, and supplying to, the same person and therefore at any given moment you will owe them money and they will owe you also. In these circumstances, there is obviously some benefit to be obtained by making a contra entry in your books and their books, setting one off against the other. In its simplest form, if you owe someone £100 and that person owes you £100, then rather than issuing cheques for £100 you can both agree to set off the balances and neither of you will owe anything.

It is rarely as simple as that and there are difficulties. Firstly, the contra agreement should always be in writing so that both parties know precisely what is being contra-ed and what is not, particularly since it is unlikely that both parties will owe exactly the same amount of money and the contra agreement will probably take the form of a balancing sum in addition. In other words, if you owe the other party £100 and they owe you £75, then you can agree to a contra of £75 and you can pay them £25, clearing both debts. Since this sort of agreement is prone to dispute at a later date, and since otherwise the documentation is not in place, this should always be effected in writing and reflected on any statements issued. In addition, you should ensure that the same contras have appeared on statements issued by the other party to you.

Secondly, a further complication comes in the declaration of VAT, particularly where you are on a 'cash accounting scheme'. On this scheme, you account for VAT on sales when the monies are received and it would be easy to overlook declaring the VAT on a debt cleared by contra. This would constitute an offence as you would be failing to declare properly the amount of due VAT payable to the Customs & Excise, as the contra is as good as cash received.

VAT apart, contra entries also have a habit of upsetting even the best book-keeping systems and you might possibly wish to avoid them for this reason alone.

Contra entries eliminate the risk of one party paying and then not getting paid by the other; it's a good time to be honest with yourself and ask who the bad payer was likely to be!

- **It is all too easy to agree to contra entries verbally; always ensure that written agreement is obtained.**

[ 66 ]

## RETENTION OF TITLE AND GOODS ON CONSIGNMENT

'Possession is nine points of the law.' (Proverb)

In the ordinary course of business, when your customer receives the goods you have despatched, title passes to the latter, i.e. they become his or her legal property. You then have a legal claim on the money which is then owed to you.

Recovery of the debt is then based on a claim against the net assets of the business, which more often than not are little or nothing.

You may be able to protect yourself to some degree by retaining title to the goods, i.e. you remain the owner of the goods even after they have been delivered to your customer until such time as they have been paid for, at which point title then transfers to the latter. It's a bit like handing over the goods whilst keeping your fingers crossed behind your back! In the event of recovery, you will then be able to take back the goods that have been handed to your customer ahead of the claims of others.

In order to do this you would have to specify a retention of title clause in your contracts, invoices, and other documents. It would be advisable for this to be drawn up by your solicitor.

The clause should also specify that your customer has a duty to store the goods in an easily recognisable location and also to maintain them in good order.

Despite the increase in use of retention of title clauses, it has to be admitted that there are more holes in the system than in the Channel tunnel. Enforcement of the clauses of these contracts is far from satisfactory, particularly as the customer may well have used your goods in some manufacturing process along with the goods of others, who also have retention of title clauses, making clear identification of your products impossible. (Imagine walking into a warehouse full of squeaky rubber Bugs Bunny toys and shrieking 'But the blue paint powder is *mine!'*) Usually what will happen is that the courts will find in your favour and you will have judgment on your side, but recovery is another matter.

It is probably still a useful idea to consider, as it costs little to make this a standard clause in your contracts. It is as close as you can come to retaining the goods while still handing them to a third party.

Goods on consignment, or 'sale or return', is another way of passing over the physical possession of goods to your customer but retaining legal title yourself. In these situations, the customer must pay you for goods purchased from you at the point when they are sold on to someone else; any goods not sold are then still legally yours and can be recovered by you.

This sort of arrangement is obviously very beneficial to your customers, who will effectively not have to buy the goods until they have already sold them, giving them an enormous cashflow advantage. Nothing is for nothing, however, and the enormous cashflow advantage to them is an obvious disadvantage to you, but one which may be worth considering if it both brings in business that you would not otherwise have and also gives some protection over loss of stock.

This type of arrangement is normal in certain industries particularly in the retail of books or magazines, where the retailer has a guaranteed right to return unsold stocks. I remember talking to someone involved in the sale of a book that came out on the day Laker airlines collapsed; its opening line was 'What makes Freddie Laker so successful'. . . .

- **Retaining title to goods is an easy way of establishing a priority claim if your debtor becomes insolvent.**

## LARGE COMPANIES THAT DELIBERATELY DELAY PAYMENTS

'With the great part of rich people, the chief employment of riches consists in the parade of riches.' (Adam Smith)

The extent to which one company can pressurise another company into prompt payment of debts amounts in the end to the degree of 'clout' that can be exercised.

It is a general rule that large companies are obviously less susceptible to pressure than small companies because, simply, they have plenty of people clamouring to do business with them. They are not dependent on any one individual in the same way that smaller companies are.

Certainly many large companies have a deliberate policy of delaying payment of their debts long beyond agreed credit term periods and of refusing to accept interest charges. Their clout is usually greater than that of those they are dealing with.

For that reason, dealing with large companies, particularly if you are small or medium sized, can be a mixed blessing. There are obvious advantages in the potential large volume of business and clearly they are generally a less risky proposition with regard to eventually getting paid. There are clear disadvantages: you become at their mercy and will often be expected to alter many of your own working procedures to suit theirs. They will often insist on top class treatment (even while giving you third class treatment) and sometimes you will find this is to the detriment of your ability to serve your other customers. Another obvious disadvantage is that there will be others like you competing for a large share of the market and there will be the occasional price-cutting war designed to elbow you out and them in, which will probably mean you will be forced to reduce your profit margins. In a very short time, small businesses dealing with such large companies find themselves operating at so reduced a profit that they cannot financially continue and they may have reached that stage having already lost some smaller, possibly sounder, business.

All the considerations for making a decision as to whether to do business with large companies are beyond the scope of this book, but the effect of their inability to be pressured by you if you are a smaller business certainly is, and should not be under-estimated. To give an example of this:

Let us suppose that you have many customers all paying promptly on one month credit given. Your total sales in the year are £120,000, therefore £10,000 per month. We will assume that the rate of interest is 15%. Net profit is £9,600, i.e. 8% of sales.

At any given time you will be financing one month's sales, probably by borrowing that much money from the bank, i.e. a constant overdraft of £10,000 which at 15% will be costing you £1,500 per year.

Now let us suppose that you decide to change your trading pattern, having been offered a contract with one large company who will take £120,000 sales from you per year at £10,000 per month, i.e. exactly the same basic trading pattern as before. Bear in mind that no basic figures have been changed, i.e. you are still making the same sales and, ignoring interest charges, the same profits. However, this company then takes four months to pay its debts.

On this basis you will then be financing not £10,000 constantly, but £40,000 constantly, and you will have to borrow this from the bank at 15% which will cost you £6,000 p.a.

Now your net profit is £5,100 (i.e. the £9,600 you had

before less the additional interest of £4,500 you are now incurring) which represents 4.25% net profit on sales instead of the 8% that you were recovering.

In addition to this, you may have obtained your £10,000 loan on an unsecured basis, whereas almost certainly with a turnover of £120,000 you would be expected to provide substantial security for a loan of £40,000 and this may involve putting your personal assets, i.e. your house, at risk.

You might argue that your previous customers could also take liberties with the credit period and have the same effect, but this is most unlikely. Many customers will not act as a single unit. They will not have the clout against you that a large company has, and the loss of one or two bad payers – at your own insistence – will not damage you in the way that losing your only customer would.

The fact is that large companies gain considerable wealth by forcing other people to do their borrowing for them; know this when deciding if you want to be one of them.

This example serves to show the wisdom of good credit control, a subject which is covered in other sections. For the purpose of this section, it can be regarded as a realistic and everyday problem of dealing with large companies and one which the small businessman should consider strongly before accepting what may seem to be a lucrative offer.

To reiterate the previous point, you will then be at the mercy of this one major client and if there is competition for their custom you may find yourself having to squeeze your gross profit margins, i.e. sell at a slightly reduced amount though saving nothing on your purchasing, and in a very short time your 8% profit will become a 0% profit or a loss.

And there is only one end to a company which sets out to make losses!

- **The big guy always wins, but only if he has the element of surprise. If you decide to go in, at least do it with knowledge.**

## RECOGNISING AND COUNTERACTING THE EXCUSES

> 'Much truth is spoken, that more may be concealed.'
> (Lord Darling)

While not often responsible for great works of fiction, many accounts departments of companies faced with having to explain why they are not paying your invoice show an ability that, if properly channelled, would compete with the fantasies of H. G. Wells.

To list them all, or even to try, would be pointless, but there are some things you can do which, if they do not get over the immediate problem, may at least deter the excuses in future. We will look at those shortly, but in the meantime remember that excuses are only excuses and should be treated as such. Under no circumstances believe what you are told, even if the excuse occasionally also happens to be the truth.

One company that I acted for as external auditor had what was called a 'top hat' column in its aged creditor listing, i.e. its analysis of what bills it had to pay. When I asked what the top hat was, it was explained to me by the MD that there was no way the company could afford to pay all its bills, so it had adopted the policy of a meta-phorical 'top hat'. The MD envisaged it was sitting on his desk and into it he would throw all the bills he thought he had to pay; from this he would select the ones he was actually going to pay. The point he made was that those

suppliers who didn't cause him any trouble didn't even get in the top hat in the first place, let alone get picked for payment from it! Your job therefore is to counter the excuses and be a nuisance, so at least you get yourself into the top hat.

The precise steps you take will depend on the amount of the debt and therefore its importance in collection. Large debts obviously will be pursued more vigorously than small ones, but the following are some possibilities:

*'You didn't send us an invoice.'*

Immediately send a copy invoice by Recorded Delivery, addressing it to a particular person in the customer's accounts department. It will not hurt if you make some fuss in order to obtain that person's name, you will certainly be remembered. If you have fax facilities, then immediately send a fax, again addressed to a specific person, and ask on the fax for a fax back confirming receipt. If you do not receive it very shortly, ring up again and ask them to fax back a receipt then. All of this fuss will cause the company time and effort and should at least ensure that you won't be left out of the top hat in future. It may also be a good idea, in future, to send the invoice along with the goods, so that if they have received the goods they can hardly claim not to have received the invoice. In this case the excuse will probably evolve into 'We have lost your invoice', in which case you go back to the start (do not pass go and do not collect £200!)

*'We only pay on statement and you have not sent us one'* (or *'We have lost it'* etc., etc.)

Procedure for this must be the same as above, but in future ensure that statements are sent promptly, possibly along with each invoice or immediately following it.

*'We do not agree the amounts on your statement/invoice.'*

Do not let this one become an excuse for allowing your invoices and statements to flounder in somebody else's in-tray. Tie up their accounts department's time by dealing with the queries over the telephone, even if this means a long and protracted procedure. It will be a nuisance to them and, if it is just an excuse, it is unlikely to

[ 74 ]

resurface again, so the time taken on your part may be well spent. In the event that this is not an excuse but a real reason, then it also means it will be dealt with promptly, which it will never be by post.

*'We did not receive the goods'* (or *'They were not what we ordered'* or *'They were damaged,'* etc., etc.)

Dealing with this particular complaint in the first instance may mean a lot of time-consuming unravelling to ensure that the goods were actually delivered and were correct. You should point out that by now probably 30 or 60 days have passed, whereas in fact they should have contacted you more promptly about this. The lesson here is one for the future; make sure particularly with this company (and indeed you should make it a policy in any case) that you have the proper documentation, i.e. signed delivery notes, to ensure that you can name the person who has accepted the goods and confirmed them to be in proper condition.

*'Our accounts are with our accountants/auditors.'*

This is a very common one, and an outrageous lie! As an external auditor and accountant to many businesses, I know that it is simply not the way 'the system' works for this to occur. In the case of large companies, the source documents almost never leave the client's premises, the auditor goes to them. In the case of smaller companies, the auditor will always make sure that if he has to take currently active documentation away from the premises in order to perform the audit, he will in fact certify copies himself and take the copies, leaving the original documents with the client. In any event, most companies do not send their accounts off to the auditors until several months after the year-end have passed, by which time these matters ought to have already been sorted out. Since many companies operate on computer systems or loose-leaf books, the auditors are usually presented with only those sheets applicable to the year in question and the company retains the current working papers. Where this is not so, the auditor would not leave the client without their source books for a long period of time, because the company would not be able to function in other fields without them.

I did once receive a very excited phone call from one of my client's creditors who was seeking payment from my client, blaming me in no uncertain terms for the delay in payment because it had been explained to her that I was holding all the necessary records and there was nothing my client could do. I fielded the telephone call somewhat diplomatically, referring her back to the client, and in the meantime telephoned the client and explained to *him* (in equally excited terms) why I did not want to be put in that position again – particularly as in this case we did not even have any of his records, as the audit wasn't even due!

This one is therefore always an excuse and never the truth. If you receive it, telephone the MD and point out some of the arguments above; there is at least a reasonable chance that the MD will contact the accounts department and ask them to deal with it, because he doesn't want those kind of phone calls again. Of course, the accounts department will probably be operating on the MD's instructions but you are far more likely to be in the top hat next month than otherwise.

*'We are having our VAT control visit.'*

VAT control visits take place on the client's premises and do not prevent the client from getting to his papers. On the other hand there are occasions when the VAT man exhibits what would appear to be the training he has received from a two-week intensive course with the SAS, swinging in through the client's windows at six o'clock in the morning and taking all the papers away. This is only done in very extreme circumstances and if it has happened to your customer, it suggests more than a mere hiccup. Probably your best course of action is to start considering how to account for bad debts in your books!

And you won't go in the top hat next month either, because the VAT man will have sold it to recover his debts, and he's preferential, you're not.

*'The last statement we received from you did not show the payment we had made to you.'*

The answer to this is, 'If you had paid us more promptly last month, it would have done!'

*'We are rearranging our offices and there is some hold-up with the paperwork.'*

Fine. This can happen once, do not let it become a regular excuse and in this case regular means twice! I recall once, relating to supply of goods rather than payment of debts, being told several times on different occasions that 'the van has broken down in Reading.' I would have minded less if they had offered some variation on where the van had broken down; if you are going to be lied to, at least let it be by a professional!

*'All our accounts are paid at each month end.'*

This one has the best chance of actually being true, as many companies are becoming heavily dependent on computers and regular planned print-outs which instruct it on its actions. However, you should know this after the first month or so and be planning for it. In that case if you are chasing them, it may well be because last month-end you did not receive your cheque, in which case the excuse becomes invalid (i.e. you didn't get into the top hat). It will depend on the amount of clout that you have as to whether you can force them into a sub-system of their computer routine and get them to pay mid-month or whether you will have to adapt yourself to their payment schedules. Bear in mind that all companies, where susceptible to pressure, can always break out of established routines if they want to.

*'Your cheque is in the post.'*

Unfortunately, your post is in the Royal Mail hold of the SS Titanic and you'll receive it 'when your ship comes in'. Those who wait for their ship to come in usually find they're at the airport when it does. More than once and this one is so unimaginative it is insulting, so the best response is simply 'I don't believe you.' Of course, you will have to accept it the first time round, but remember that the second time round the answer will always be 'That's what you said last time, and it wasn't.' Go on the attack!

All the above answers to these rather sorry excuses have the one major drawback that they cost you time and effort and this is time and effort you would rather spend making more, and more productive, sales. It may be time well spent if it ensures you get into the top hat next month and these excuses can be left to be directed at those more receptive to them than you.

There are two other considerations:

1.  Where more major clients are concerned, look at the specific arrangements which they have and be pre-

pared to modify your own position to accept them. Build the additional cost of servicing those clients into your costing framework and do not spend additional time worrying about what you cannot change. If the cost or the problems involved are unacceptable, then look for business elsewhere.

2. A reasonable appeal will not fall on deaf ears if your customer wishes to enjoy a good relationship with you and is not desperately struggling to pay bills.

Write a letter directly to the MD of the company, setting out the difficulties that the company is causing you personally and asking them to negotiate with you a more suitable arrangement. In many cases this will work and indeed it will be adhered to.

A reasonable appeal is obviously preferable to a threat, but eventually a threat may be required. In that case one approach might be a Recorded Delivery letter directly to the home of the managing director, which has a certain psychological shock value. The addresses of company directors can be obtained from the public file at the Companies Registry which can be accessed either by going there in person, requesting a 'search' by post, or using a search agency, for a nominal fee. (Addresses of search agencies can be found in the Yellow Pages.) All limited companies have a statutory obligation to file such records, though no such obligation exists for unincorporated businesses.

- **If someone takes advantage of you once, it reflects badly on them; if they take advantage of you twice, it reflects badly on you.**

# SECTION 3

# HOW TO RECOVER BAD DEBTS

## WHICH DEBTS TO TACKLE FIRST

'Saturday's child works hard for his living.'
(Nursery Rhyme)

When most companies analyse their debts, they find
that a very small percentage of customers account for a
very large percentage of the outstanding amount. (Don't
they say it's just a few hooligans on the terraces that
make all the trouble at the football match?) In other
words, there are some very large debts and a lot of very
small ones. It may well be easiest to collect the smaller
ones, particularly as they will cause your debtors less
trouble to pay them, but this is just taking the soft option;
effective debt control demands that you concentrate on
what is important rather than what is easy. In other
words, you must pursue the big debts first. If you have
time to pursue them all, then all well and good but if not,
then this will ensure that you are taking the most
effective action.

All this may seem very obvious, but the truth is that
most companies, particularly small companies where the
sole proprietor is overworked anyway, tend to try to cure
the easiest rather than the biggest problems. Having got

some results, they then pat themselves on the back (no easy manoeuvre) and ignore the fact that they are not taking effective action. Their limited successes are masking the underlying reality.

Never chase ten pence with a pound; obviously any debt collection must be proportionate to the money being recovered and very small debts probably do not merit any effort whatsoever. If such debts arise from underpayment of invoices, then they probably will be paid if you issue a statement picking up the amount when the next invoices go out. However, they should never arise from specific invoices – there is an effective minimum below which credit should not be given for practical reasons (see Section Two page 35).

- **Getting the most money in is what counts, not the number of debts collected.**

## HOW TO WRITE 'RECOVERY' LETTERS

'I think it's good for a writer to think he's dying; he works harder.' (Tennessee Williams)

The idea of a recovery letter is to collect in your debt as quickly as possible and with a minimum of fuss. It is *not* designed to wish your debtors well in the future, to ask how their children are getting on and so on. Rudeness would certainly be counter-productive, but brevity will equal bluntness and firmness and both of these are part of the 'short sharp shock' that helps persuade debtors that the time to pay up has come. Avoid, then, convoluted sentences; use short simple words in a very short simple letter. It is not a literary work of art, you are not competing for the Booker Prize; just tell your debtor that you want payment. If you feel the need to elaborate further, then tell him or her you want payment *now*!

[ 84 ]

Your letter should be concise; it should explain exactly how much money you are demanding and exactly why you are demanding it. If there is any question as to the address to which the remittance should be sent, then this should be specified in the body of the letter.

As an aid to persuasion, it may help to explain to your debtor what steps you are proposing to take if he or she does not pay up. Refer where necessary to legislation in support of your actions, i.e. if you are writing because an earlier cheque has bounced, then point out that the 1968 Theft Act makes it a criminal offence to issue a cheque, knowing that insufficient funds are available to cover it. You might also make reference to other impending legal action.

Debtor situations which require letters to follow them up invariably mean there is some deterioration in the relationship between yourself and your customer. A well handled approach and satisfactory resolution to the problem can in fact further cement a good relationship, so you might at this point look on your debtor as an *opportunity* rather than a problem. To this end, your letter should always be courteous, as this will be appreciated in future dealings. Having said that, your letter should never contain any form of hesitation or apology: you have every right to ask for your money and if an apology is due, it is due *to* you, not from you.

Your demand must not only be firm and concise, but must be unwavering; do not suggest that if your debtor cannot afford the full amount, they should pay a reduced amount. By doing so, you will absolutely guarantee yourself a reduced payment. In this case you will have literally asked for it!

Also, do not bother asking why your debt has not been paid because you will be inviting a useless and probably pathetic excuse which is of no value to you. Your lack of interest in why you have not been paid is more expressive, correctly reflecting the fact that you are not interested in why you have not been paid, only that you should now be paid without further delay.

If you threaten any action such as handing the matter over to your solicitor or applying to the County Court, then follow it through if the debt is not paid. Never fail to follow through a threat or you will lose credibility and strength in your arguments. Worse still, you will encourage your debtor to continue not to pay you. Certainly when you have had to reach this stage with any debtor, there should be no question of extending further credit in the future and all future work should either be done by deposits in advance or cash on delivery.

Having attacked with a few sticks, offer the debtor some carrots: reasons why they will be better off paying the debts than not paying them. You should point out that if you do have to take legal action, it may damage their credit-worthiness and therefore their future business dealings with many customers, not only yourself. If they value your business, then payment of a debt will enable you to continue to trade with each other. Furthermore, payment of the debt will mean that you will be more likely to extend credit to them in the future and you will not be restricting them to cash terms or payments in advance. (However, you will not be bound by this when the time to consider fresh credit comes in the future and if you feel that recovery, albeit successful, was an unwelcome difficulty you may still 'pull the plug' and restrict credit. However, there is no point mentioning that at this stage.) You might also point out that legal action, even if the debt is not recovered, will involve your debtor in considerable time and effort and probably further costs of their own.

By the time you reach the stage of recovery letters, it

may be advisable to consider writing to the main directors of the company, who will then have to take some sort of positive action in instructing their staff what to do with your debt. Go for the jugular; for maximum psychological impact, it can be a good idea to write to the directors at their home addresses, as already suggested (see p. 80). It is remarkable how threatened directors feel when even innocuous letters arrive at their home addresses and they are consequently much more likely to do something positive about getting rid of that threat.

Your letter must always have the appearance of being an individually prepared letter and not a preprinted form. Any preprinted document will look as if cartons of them are being despatched by the boatload and therefore you will not be following it up, as it is just 'a routine' to go through. Individual letters look as if they *will* be followed up, so make sure that they are. With the use of modern word processors you can have 'individual' letters stored as a template in the word processor, so that each debt recovery letter can be made to look personalised with the minimum of effort. One particular point to be added to any individually targeted letter is a reference to previous letters which have been sent and presumably were unanswered, or at least not complied with. This not only adds to the individuality of the letter being received, but makes clear that you are indeed monitoring the situation very closely.

One failing of many credit control departments is the use of expressions such as 'First demand' or 'First reminder'. These should be avoided *at all costs*, as the use of the word 'first' implies that there will be a second and possibly even a third, etc. Receiving a demand with 'First reminder' written on it means you can safely drop it in the in-tray, or file it carefully in the wastepaper basket, while you wait for the second; the first reminder was therefore totally useless and a waste of time. Your letter must have urgency about it.

In the same way, do not use the expression 'Final demand' unless you are truly planning then to take legal action. To use the expression 'Final demand' closes off your own avenues for further demands and loses you all credibility if you then have to make further demands or fail to follow up your 'Final demand'. There is a limit anyway to how many letters you can write, probably two and certainly three. Beyond that point, your debtor will become quite comfortable with filing your letter in the wastepaper basket as a matter of routine. If three letters have not succeeded, then alternative action is required.

- **Be polite – be brief – be firm.**

## DEBT COLLECTION BY TELEPHONE

> 'The new electronic interdependence recreates the world in the image of a global village.' (Marshall McLuhan)

Telephone conversations should not be used as a first resort as they are expensive compared with letters, which are the first line of attack. Telephone conversations tie your own staff up for extended periods and staff time costs money; in addition, telephone calls are themselves relatively expensive.

However, when telephone collection is required there are certain rules to follow. Firstly, find out who it is that is responsible for paying your debt and talk to that particular individual directly by name, giving your own name and thereby putting him or her at the disadvantage of having to deal with a person rather than a faceless corporation.

Record your conversation as there may be particular points raised which you can use against the person concerned in future correspondence; don't for a minute consider this to be an unfair tactic – the Geneva convention has not been extended to debt collection and in any case they have enough advantages on their side already (i.e. your money!).

Before you speak to the person, ensure that you are fully ready for the conversation. If you are well prepared, then you will not have to keep breaking off to go to files for past correspondences or copies of invoices, and so on. The main reason for this is that you can hammer home your demand without giving your debtor breathing space to think up new excuses. Have on your desk copies of all invoices, statements, correspondence, details relating to their credit status and so on. Know where each document is so that you can lay hands on it very quickly and do not be afraid to counter any statement they make with proof. When all else fails, use the facts!

Be sure that you know precisely what the debt is you are asking for. If they say, 'but we paid you £1,000 last month and I am sure that covered the invoice you are talking about', be sure that you can *immediately* reply 'No, that paid invoices such and such, leaving this invoice still outstanding.' Give the numbers of the invoices paid and the ones outstanding, so be sure to have their debtor ledger sheets with you.

Before calling, be prepared to counter the more obvious excuses; be ready with your responses. There are very few that they can offer that are valid; 'We think we have already paid you' (be precise in your planned response); 'We are having bad cashflow problems at the present time' (your response might well point out, politely but firmly, that financing their working capital is their bank's responsibility and not yours).

Excuses such as 'The wife's in hospital', 'My kids have got chickenpox', 'My grandmother just died', and the like, need only the response 'I am very sorry to hear it, but let's keep to the point at hand which is the collection of my debt'. Make that one sentence and not two which will emphasise the irrelevance of the excuse and your dismissal of it; they have probably buried more grand-mothers in their time than you have had hot dinners.

Since the debtor cannot physically pay you over the telephone, then the best you can possibly get in a normal course of events is a firm commitment to be paid on a specific date. Ensure that you get this from the telephone conversation and make a record of it in the file. On the specific date and no later, follow up the lack of receipt if that is the case.

Be prepared to go on the attack and use the element of surprise when necessary. One particular response you will frequently get is 'Your cheque is in the post', in which case *immediately* ask precisely what the date and number of the cheque is, ensure that it is for the full amount of the debt and straight away challenge if it is not. If your debtor wavers at all in his responses, then it probably indicates that he has not written the cheque out yet. If he has a habit of telling you your cheque is in the post and has not arrived, do not be afraid to point this out to him at this stage; indeed, with firmness and politeness, do not be afraid to suggest that his past record makes it difficult for you to believe him. The more battered and bruised he feels when he comes off the tele-phone, the more likely he is to 'pay you off'.

Be ready to surprise your debtor even further: if he states that he will have his cheque ready tomorrow for posting then, if practical, immediately respond that he is not to post it, but you will come down and pick it up from him in person. This may back him into a position of issuing a cheque he hadn't intended to and you will then have some evidence for an impending court case, to say nothing of possibly a bounced cheque which you can hold against him in a letter pointing out the terms of the Theft Act. And you never know, he might accidentally have left enough money in his account to pay you.

The worst possibility that can arise from this is that you will get there and find that unfortunately he had to go out at the last minute and 'must have forgotten your cheque'. Because of this ploy, don't commit yourself to any lengthy journeys or inconvenient times, but restrict this particular line of attack to easy-to-make visits.

One point to remember: if your debtor continually cannot be found, cannot come to the phone, is always in meetings, went up with the last space shuttle or is for some other reason always unable to talk to you, do not think that this means you have been unable to talk to him. It does, as they say, say more about him than cash ever can! Move on immediately to the next stage; he has said all he is going to say.

- **Be well prepared for telephone conversations. Never make them on the spur of the moment.**

## USES OF TELEX AND FAX MACHINES

'A verbal contract isn't worth the paper it's written on.' (Samuel Goldwyn)

The telex, now largely a thing of the past, is a sort of typed version of a telephone conversation and consists of sending a typed letter down a telephone line. Fax is

[ 91 ]

the more common, more modern, 'version' of telex. It consists of transmitting any image down a telephone line, rather in the manner of making a photocopy, but where the photocopy comes out at another location instead of your own.

The advantage of sending debt collection letters by fax or telex is that they have a sense of immediacy at the receiving end and indeed all faxes and telexes at present tend to be dealt with more speedily than 'ordinary' letters.

There are other more subtle advantages such as the fact that the letter arrives at the receiving end open for all to see and it may well be that the proprietors do not want their staff to know that they are having trouble paying their debts and they will not appreciate your telex or fax giving the game away.

That the fax or telex creates a written record may well be useful in future action.

One particular offensive use of the fax is that if your debtors tell you that your cheque is in the post, you can ask them to fax a copy of the counterfoil, on the basis that they have said that before and it has not always been entirely accurate. (If they tell you the counterfoil won't fit in the fax machine, tell them to photocopy it and transmit the photocopy.) This is hardly a foolproof method, but it has shock offensive tactics to it and anything which leaves the debtors feeling that they will be better off without you chasing their tail will work to your advantage.

- **Fax machines and telex are still an immediate means of communicating; use them for greater impact.**

## PERSONAL APPEARANCES

'Don't fire until you see the whites of their eyes.'
(William Prescott)

This is the least cost effective method of debt collection, though it can get results. It involves a great deal of time and difficulty, but its main disadvantage is that many people feel unable to confront others effectively or feel that they will lose 'face' if they do not come away with a cheque or at least a meeting with the appropriate person. It should not be used unless other methods of collection have failed, but when used a few lessons from the SAS may be in order.

Although it is not necessary to machine-gun your way through a brick wall, it is best to arrive unexpectedly to avoid giving your debtor a chance to 'leave suddenly'. In large companies this may not be completely effective, as the person you want will be insulated by receptionists and secretaries and possibly you will fail to get through, but in small companies the proprietor can usually be found in his or her office or workshop and confronted directly.

The usual debt collection rules apply: you should be firm, courteous but unwavering in your demand. All you want to come away with is a cheque in full settlement of your debt and nothing else will do.

Physically handing over a cheque from one person to another eliminates all the excuses such as 'lost in the post', 'got interrupted shortly after the telephone call and forgot to write out the cheque', 'got run over by a herd of zebras in the car park', and so on. Therefore a failure to receive a cheque when you make a personal visit is a very strong indication that your debtor is planning not to pay you. Take swift and extreme action *immediately* as there is no point wasting further time receiving more refusals.

If the person you are looking for will not see you or refuses to make himself available, then he has surely told you all you need to know. Do not delay – drop into your solicitors or the County Court on your way back!

- **Confrontation is best handled with calmness and strength; never lose your head.**

## DEBT COLLECTION AGENCIES

'War hath no fury like a non-combatant.' (C. E. Montague)

For a great many reasons, debt collection agencies *can* be a very effective method of debt collection. This is a pity in a way, because the problem for you is that many debt collection agencies do not get results and the worst are charlatans.

The advantage they have is that they concentrate on this one specific activity and they are not pressured by the other considerations of running your business as you are. In addition, they are experienced in fending off excuses, pressing home the urgency of the demand, and so on. Furthermore, because they are a third party they have the psychological effect of being one more exposure of the debtor's bad credit-worthiness, and because of their position there is always the implied threat that knowledge of the debtor's poor finances will extend to other potential suppliers.

Do not be afraid that they will harm your image; remember they are only exposing themselves to people who are already causing you harm, not your good customers.

[ 94 ]

Because of the charlatans entering the field, you should always ensure that your debt collection agency is properly registered. You should obtain references on them – particularly from existing clients of their practice – and you should make sure that you are aware of the precise terms of the contract you have with them.

One particular 'dodge' that some debt collection agencies are using is ineffective pursuit of debts followed by very swift threats of legal action and you will be expected to foot the legal bills incurred by *their* in-house solicitors. They exist almost as a front for highly expensive legal departments, and this is where their profits lie.

Another possibility to be avoided is any form of payment up front or a flat fee regardless of recovery; good collection agencies will only ever charge on the basis of percentage of debts actually recovered. If they don't do their work well, then you should not have to pay them.

Debt collection agencies are of course skilled at 'attacking' your debtor without crossing the legal boundaries. This is another advantage to you in that you may not be fully aware of precisely what the law does and does not allow, while at the same time the greater your debtors feel under threat, the more likely they are to pay the money.

An 18 stone, 6ft. 4in. homicidal maniac with a stocking over his head and a very large axe in his hands, weaving his way through your debtor's premises smashing all and sundry and shouting 'Gimme money!' is highly likely to be an effective debt collector but, perhaps sadly from your point of view, quite illegal.

- **Debt collectors can be a great help, but you will have to choose very carefully.**

[ 95 ]

## SOLICITORS

'I do not care to speak ill of any man behind his back, but I believe the gentleman is an attorney.' (Samuel Johnson)

Solicitors have certain uses in debt collection; for a nominal sum of a few pounds, they can issue a simple letter to your debtor threatening legal action and this alone often has the desired effect.

If not paid, in the case of small debts, it is probably best if you then follow this up with a private County Court action (see section 4 in this book) rather than instruct your solicitor to take it up, as legal costs will be prohibitory.

With regard to using solicitors as debt collectors; generally, they are about as much good as a chocolate teapot. Firstly, they will charge high professional fees whether they succeed or not, and the very fact of their receiving their money come win or lose makes them less enthusiastic than other debt collection agencies.

Furthermore, solicitors are not able to follow up their threats with such tactics as personal appearances, as they do not have time for this and probably many of them regard it as beneath their personal dignity.

If you really feel inclined to use solicitors, then find one who claims to be a specialist, give him or her one debt to collect and monitor their work very closely. If you are pleased with it, then by all means continue, but be prepared to be disappointed.

- **Despite appearances, solicitors are not really suitable for the job.**


## POST-DATED CHEQUES

'Time is a great teacher, but unfortunately it kills all its pupils.' (Hector Berlioz)

Post-dated cheques are marginally better than the promise of payment at a later time, but only marginally so!

If the debtor has no funds to pay you now, then there is no guarantee they will have funds to pay you when the post-dated cheques become due and if not, the bank will not honour the cheques. Nevertheless, they do have certain advantages; firstly, they put the point of payment into your hands, rather than relying on your debtor sending you a cheque at the appropriate time; secondly, if it comes to a court case, they represent evidence of acceptance of debt in the same way as any other cheque.

And of course, an amazing thing might happen: they might actually clear the bank and you will have your money!

If post-dated cheques bounce, then deal with them as you would any other bouncing cheque, and as promptly as possible. If you fear there is some doubt that they will be cleared, then it may even be an advantage to remind your debtor in writing shortly before presentation that you are presenting the cheques and that funds should be in the bank. You might casually throw in a reminder of the terms of the 1968 Theft Act, which makes it a criminal offence to issue a cheque if you know that you do not have money in the bank to cover it.

When negotiating to accept post-dated cheques, the rule must be to negotiate as short a time as possible; obviously because quick collection is best for your cash flow, but also because as time goes by clients who are in difficulty only sink deeper into the quicksand.

The quicker you can dislodge their hand from around your ankle, the more chance you have of not being sucked down with them!

- **Take post-dated cheques rather than nothing, but they are an extension to the credit period — make it as short as possible.**

## PART PAYMENTS

'A bird in the hand is worth two in the bush.' (Proverb)

Given the wisdom of the above proverb, accept a part payment rather than no payment at all – but only on certain terms. Your debtor may be genuinely trying to pay off all debts and therefore making part payments to all creditors. If you believe your debtor is sincere, then it may be worth extending the credit period for part of the debt in exchange for a part payment now.

This is, however, by arrangement and it is up to you whether you accept it or not. If your debtor simply makes a part payment with no agreement between you both, then you should not consider that this leaves you with any obligations. You should simply proceed with your normal and vigorous debt collection of the remaining balance.

It also stands to reason that should your debtor pay off part of the debt and then ask for a similar amount of credit to be extended again, you should refuse this without hesitation. Nor should you negotiate even part payments on this basis. To do so would simply be extending the degree to which you are financing them, and prolonging an inevitable bad debt in the end. Better to put them out of your misery.

- **Part payments should only be by mutual agreement, if not then you move to collect the rest of the debt immediately.**

## MORATORIUMS

'The future is made of the same stuff as the present.' (Simone Weil)

A moratorium is a rather grand word for simply a pause or a delay.

If a business discovers that its working capital is so

restricted that it cannot pay its debts and cannot foresee in the normal course of events that it is likely to be able to, then it can ask its collected creditors for a moratorium, i.e. a pause for a certain period during which time the company sorts itself out.

Theoretically a moratorium could be called if the company simply felt that in the course of normal trading it would have more money available to pay its debts in future months. But this is rarely the case and moratoriums usually refer to more serious reorganisations on the company's part.

If approached by your debtor and asked to accept a moratorium, then it would certainly be unwise simply to accept the company's assurances that 'things will be better later', as this is more likely to reflect the wishful thinking of the proprietor than any reasoned financial analysis. Acceptable moratoriums usually mean that the company will spend an agreed period of time drawing in finance by exceptional means, such as cheap sales of the stock and possibly even sales of some fixed assets, realisation of investments, and so on.

Although informal, moratoriums should be recorded in writing. It may be worthwhile instructing your solicitor to examine the documentation to ensure that your debt is protected and also that the company will report to you at periodic stages in order to let you know that it is successfully realising its assets and producing the cash needed to pay your, and other, debts.

- **Don't let moratoriums go unsupervised by you. It's your money they are supposed to be producing.**

## STATUTORY DEMAND

'Stand and deliver!' (Attributed to Dick Turpin)

Section 518 of the Companies Act of 1985 (amended by the Companies Act 1989) states that if you are owed in excess of £750 by a limited company and that sum is overdue, you may serve on the company a notice demanding payment within 21 days, known as a Statutory Demand. (In the case of individuals, the Statutory Demand is dealt with in this book in the section on Bankruptcy. See p. 104.) Failure to pay the debt then leaves you the option of petitioning to the High Court for the company to be wound up.

Be sure that you are going to win the action if you take it. In other words, be absolutely certain that you can support your claim with irrefutable documentation because costs in the High Court are very high and if you fail in the action, then they will be awarded against you.

If you have prepared your case correctly, then the advantage of this form of debt collection is that it is very fast and guaranteed to produce a high-level and immediate response from officials of the company.

- **Make sure you have a watertight case before proceeding; being right in law is not enough, you have to be able to prove that you are right.**

## AVOIDING THE CHARGE OF HARASSMENT

'Ignorance of the law excuses no man: not that all men know the law, but because 'tis an excuse every man will plead.' (John Selden)

A too vigorous pursuit of your outstanding debts can take you outside the law and leave you open to charges being laid against you. There are obvious areas where this will be the case and these should be a matter of common sense. Threatening physical violence, for example, would be one such example, then there is actual physical violence which could well lead to a criminal charge. Damage to property and breaking and entering are other clear examples of where your pursuit of debts owed would be too vigorous, to put it mildly.

One particular area where the layman is not generally well versed, and where it would be easy to break the law through ignorance, would be the area of harassment. In this general field you will be under the Administration of Justice Act of 1970. It makes clear that you cannot present either yourself or false documents which suggest you are officially authorised to enforce the debt collection, nor can you threaten criminal proceedings if the debt is not paid, since non-payment of debt is a matter for the civil law rather than the criminal law.

Most importantly, and the area where transgression is easiest, you may not make of your debtors such demands as cause either them or their family concern, distress or humiliation either by their nature or their frequency. This will exclude, for example, telephoning through the night and the early hours of the morning, personal approaches of a threatening nature, especially to other members of the debtor's family, and approaches which would suggest damage or injury as a result of non-payment.

One ruse that was common before the Administration of Justice Act was for debt collection agencies to emblazon their name and purpose on the side of vans and then leave them parked outside debtors' houses in the hope of embarrassing the debtor in front of neighbours. Since this would cause humiliation, it would now almost certainly be outlawed. Determining what you can and can't do it is to some extent a question of reasonableness, but if you are in doubt then seek legal advice: the law is not always constructed as you would imagine. I remember answering a question on a point of law in my law classes and the lecturer replied, with the broadest grin; 'You have used common sense and reasonableness in framing your answer; you are therefore wrong.'

- **Take advice on what you may or may not do, even if it seems reasonable.**

## BANKRUPTCY

> 'Stop the world, I want to get off.' (Anthony Newley)

When the crunch comes for an individual (i.e. anyone other than incorporated companies), the end result can be a bankruptcy.

If you take your debtor to court and the courts find in your favour, then they will issue judgment against the debtor. If the debt owed to you is in excess of £750, then you can issue a bankruptcy petition against that debtor.

An alternative is to make a Statutory Demand, requesting payment of the debt within 21 days, and if this is not complied with then bankruptcy is the ultimate end anyway.

If the court agrees, then a bankruptcy order is issued and the assets of the debtor are placed in the hands of the Department of Trade, specifically the Official Receiver. At this point the debtor must submit to the Official Receiver a statement of the assets held, and liabilities owed, by him, and the Official Receiver can hold a public enquiry at which creditors can 'cross-examine' the debtor. This is not always the case and the Official Receiver may not request a public enquiry in every situation.

A meeting of creditors is then called and the decision is made on whether to make the debtor bankrupt, in which event there will be some considerable time before he can be discharged, or the creditors may accept an arrangement to receive less than the full amount of their debt, each creditor receiving an equal pro-rata figure. This latter position is more usual because it is quick and less costly.

- **Once bankruptcy proceedings begin you can**

HOW TO RECOVER BAD DEBTS

**be as certain as of anything that you will not
be receiving the full amount owed to you.**


## LIQUIDATIONS

> 'The big print giveth and the fine print taketh away.'
> (Archbishop J. Fulton Sheen)

Liquidation is the corporate form of bankruptcy and can
be of various types.

### Members' voluntary liquidations
In a member's voluntary liquidation, the directors of the
company are required to sign a Statement of Solvency
stating that all those owed money can receive their full
settlements. These forms of liquidation usually occur
because of pressure from shareholders rather than creditors. Creditors do not usually suffer as a result of a
member's voluntary liquidation, because if they were
going to, then the directors would be unable to sign the
Statement.

### Creditors' voluntary liquidation
This is a form of liquidation forced on the company by
creditors who fear that they are not going to be paid and,
of course, in this situation the directors are unable to sign
a declaration of solvency.

The directors begin a winding-up operation on the
company and call a meeting of creditors to present a list
of assets and liabilities to them, called a Statement of
Affairs. This is similar to a Balance Sheet in a normal set
of accounts, but with assets valued at the price they are
going to be sold for, rather than their cost. The creditors
will then be requested to appoint a corporate liquidator
to carry forward the winding-up of the company. Creditors have the power of vote at the creditors' voluntary

liquidation according to the size of the debt owed to them, so a person owed £100 has twice the voting power of somebody owed £50.

## Compulsory liquidation

If the creditors lodge a petition to the court for compulsory liquidation because they are unsatisfied with the creditors' voluntary liquidation, then it is the court that issues the winding-up order and appoints the Official Receiver (from the Department of Trade) to administer the company's affairs (see Receivers in this book on p. 107).

The Department of Trade may also take this opportunity to investigate whether the company has been fraudulently trading, in which case the directors could be made personally liable for the debts incurred. If the directors have acted in good faith, then they will not be liable and if there are insufficient assets to cover the debts, the creditors will lose out. I recall reading that one such enquiry had examined a fixed asset of a company described in the books as 'Fire Extinguisher Reservoir' and discovered its true identity – it was at the Managing Director's house and his wife was still swimming in it when the Inspector arrived!

If you are a creditor in such a situation, it is also worth noting that there are automatically preferred creditors ahead of you. It probably won't come as a surprise to learn that these are principally those monies owed to the government through taxes. There may also be secured or preferred creditors, often the debtors bank, who will rank ahead of general debts.

- **In most liquidations you are likely to find yourself at the back of a very long and hungry preferential queue.**

## RECEIVERS

'I don't know what effect these men will have on the enemy, but, by God, they frighten me.' (The Duke of Wellington)

Receivers are appointed by secured creditors to safeguard the assets that have been pledged as security against credit given. If your debtor has not only incurred a debt to you but has given you security, i.e. offered you a tangible support for your debt, and subsequently fails to make payment, then you can 'call in' the security. To do so you may appoint a receiver to protect the assets. If your contract with the debtor does not have provision for the appointment of a receiver, then you may apply to the courts, asking them to appoint one.

Quite often a debt is secured over the total assets of the company and the receiver then moves in to the company and runs it in order to produce the appropriate amount of money to pay the debts. For the owner of the business, the appointment of a receiver is very painful as the owners have no power to overrule the receiver, who can sell off even the fixed assets of the company to realise the debts, and even those at an exceptionally low price in order to make the sales quickly. The owner has no power to prevent this.

The receiver may also continue to run the business for as long as is necessary to obtain all the monies due, and this may include actually ordering goods on credit.

The usual result of a receivership is that the company is then put into liquidation, because the receiver is not there to run the company for the long-term but only to realise the assets and pay the debts.

It is also important to know – as a potential supplier to a receiver ordering goods, possibly on credit – that your contract will be with the receiver and not the company and the receiver is personally liable for the debts. You should therefore make the same credit status enquiries that you would have made for the company itself before extending credit. The receiver has no power to demand credit from others.

- **When giving credit to receivers, remember they are a whole new ball game – check them out as you would anyone else.**

## RECOVERING VAT ON BAD DEBTS

'In this world nothing is certain but death and taxes.'
(Benjamin Franklin)

If VAT is accounted for on other than a cash accounting scheme, then the VAT is likely to be payable to the Customs & Excise before you have received payment from your debtor. Should you fail to receive payment, then you will suffer not only the loss of the amount due to you, but also the amount you are collecting on behalf of, and have already paid to, HM Customs & Excise. Provision is made for recovery of that amount in certain circumstances.

In the case of debts due from limited companies, relief is only due if the company becomes formally insolvent at a creditor's voluntary winding-up or by order of the court.

If the company is in the hands of a receiver, then the receiver continues to run the company and bad debt relief is not available until the receievership ends, if it should result in a winding-up.

Where the debtor is an individual, partnership or other unincorporated business, then bad debt relief is only available if it becomes formally insolvent by a bankruptcy order.

To claim bad debt relief you must have already paid over the VAT to the Customs & Excise, made the supply for a consideration in money, and title to the goods must have passed to the customer. Where you have a reservation of title clause in your contract, then bad debt relief will not be available unless you formally surrender your rights under that clause to the insolvency administrators.

To obtain bad debt relief, you should obtain a form VAT 996 from the local VAT office, complete this and send it to the person in charge of the insolvency. You will probably find that that person would have written to you requesting the completion of the form, if the circumstances dictate it. It should be noted that it is not correct to obtain VAT bad debt relief by issuing a credit note.

Since the Cash Accounting Scheme was introduced on 1st October 1987, VAT on sales can now be accounted for on a 'when paid' basis, i.e. when the money is received from the debtor. Therefore any debts not received would not be accounted for and bad debt relief would become automatic. Not everybody is eligible for the cash accounting scheme: only those whose sales, excluding VAT, are less than £250,000 and providing that the Customs & Excise approve the application. This, broadly speaking, means that your returns are up to date, you have not been convicted of a VAT offence or assessed with dishonest conduct, and that the VATman's SAS hasn't come in through your windows with the dawn recently.

- **Guidance in specific cases can be obtained from the local office of HM Custom and excise (VAT office).**

# SECTION 4

# SMALL CLAIMS: PERSONAL ACTION
# IN THE COUNTY COURT

'No brilliance is needed in the law. Nothing but common sense, and relatively clean fingernails.' (John Mortimer)

For small debtor claims, it is now possible to bring an action without the need for solicitors, thus making them more cost-effective and less time-consuming. These actions are brought in the County Courts.

Most actions are not defended, and do not end up in the court itself; those that do are usually decided easily as the judge is usually able to decide on the facts presented. Few small claims are complicated by legal technicalities. The County Courts are able to handle claims not exceeding £5,000, but many of these would involve instructing solicitors. It is the smaller claims up to £500 which concern us here, as they should not involve solicitors' costs and are often settled by arbitration.

Debts under £500 automatically go to arbitration. The only costs allowed in the action are those shown on the summons, enforcement costs and costs arising from 'unreasonable conduct' by a party to the action. One of the main advantages is that solicitors' costs are not allowed, keeping these actions cost-effective. (Debts over £500 can go to arbitration, if both parties agree; in

[ 113 ]

these cases they can also agree on the inclusion or exclusion of solicitors' costs.)

Arbitration hearings are less formal than court proceedings and are not undertaken by a judge, but usually by the court registrar.

## How to sue

The courts are clogged up with cases and they take a dim view of anyone using them as anything other than a last resort. If you have not made efforts to recover your debt by other means, then even if you win your case the courts may not award you costs, regarding them as legitimately yours to suffer.

Once you have decided to sue for recovery of your debt, you must prepare the documentation. You will need the defendant's correct name and address, as papers will have to be served on him, or that of the company, whichever is appropriate. For Limited Companies papers should be served to the registered office, the address of which can be obtained from the Companies Registry (see p. 80). Other businesses should be sued at their trading address, or at the address of the owner.

Partners are jointly and severally liable for the debts of each other relating to the business, but remember it is important that you bring the action against the *business* and not one of the partners individually, in order to benefit from this. If you sue one partner and win, but he does not have any money with which to pay you, you would then not be able to sue another partner. If you win in an action against the business, however, then all partners are equally liable.

A word of warning on postal deliveries, which could equally apply to ordinary letters to your debtor. They may come back marked 'Gone away'; do not necessarily trust this as it is a common dodge for delaying, or trying to hide from legal actions. Check whether or not your debtor *is* still there before giving up. You could even write to the business next door, asking where your debtor went; you will often get an answer and more than occasionally one that says your debtor is, in fact, still there. Debtors, like the Almighty, move in a mysterious way!

When you commence to sue, you have to file with the court what is known as the 'particulars of claim', which is a simple, short explanation of how much you are claiming, and why you believe the amount is payable. It often consists of little more than a copy of the invoice or invoices against which payment is being sought. There are few formalities required, but certain basic information is requested: the name of the court in which the action will be taken (see below), the case number (allocated on issue of the summons), the name of the plaintiff (you) and the defendant (your debtor). Any contracts or other documentation can be appended. The court can provide a 'pro-forma' layout, if required.

You must provide a copy of the particulars for the court and for each defendant, in addition to your own copy.

You may also add interest to your claim, calculated at a rate that will be given to you by the Court Office, as follows: 'The plaintiff claims interest under section 69 of the County Courts Act 1984 at the rate of X per cent per annum from (start date) to (end date) being £X, and thereafter interest at the same rate up to the date of judgment.'

The court in which the action is heard is either the court of the area in which the defendant company or individual resides, or the court of the area where the contract was drawn up (which could be the area of your own office, for example.) Any county court will supply you with the appropriate court name and address.

The procedure starts with the submission to the court of a form known as a 'request', which is used as the basis of the summons. The court's fee for issue of the summons is paid at this time.

All claims for money are dealt with by what are called 'default summons' and for claims under £500 there is automatic treatment through arbitration.

The court will issue you with a plaint number, which is a reference for your case; you will need this whenever you communicate with the court.

Once the summons has been made out, it must be served on the defendant either by the court, by post, or by you in person. If returned by post, then the court's bailiff can deliver it for an additional fee.

Default actions are not listed for fixed dates, but if the amount demanded is not paid or the defendant does not respond to the summons, then judgment can be made against him, at your request, on a simple form. You can demand settlement of the debt at the same time.

If the debtor *does* respond, then what happens next depends on that response. The defendant may admit the claim (agree to pay), but ask for time to pay and give the court details of his financial situation; it is up to you to accept or not. If you do not accept, then both you and the defendant will have to see the registrar to agree terms. You do not have to attend; you can ask the registrar to deal with the matter without you being there. You must specifically ask for this, because if you simply do not turn up, then the action may be lost and it will only be re-instated after a special application is made. If you have information that shows the debtor has not been honest in declaring his financial situation, then you should attend and place this before the registrar.

The defendant may not admit your claim; he may fight

it. The court will then either arrange a hearing, arbitration or a trial.

When defence is received by the court, a pre-trial review will be arranged, or sometimes a trial or arbitration date is set straight away. The pre-trial review is designed to allow all parties to consider what next move they wish to make. In many cases the matter can even be resolved at this stage without need for further action.

If any party believes that in claims of less than £500 the matter should *not* be referred to arbitration, but tried in court, they may apply for this, though this is less usual in simple debt claims.

At the pre-trial review there is a stage of the action known as 'discovery', where each party discloses the documents that will be used at the trial, and 'swaps' copies with each other. This makes the trial more efficient.

If the pre-trial review cannot settle the matter, then a trial date or arbitration date is set.

**Preparing your case**
You must be ready to provide the judge with evidence of your case. The fact that you know that you are right – or even that common sense dictates that you are right – is not enough; they don't say the law is an ass for nothing. The judge is not there to administer 'natural' justice; the case must be proven and bad preparation can mean a case loses, not because it is wrong, but merely because it is badly presented.

Evidence given at an arbitration hearing is less formal than in court. The only rules to remember are to try to order your presentation so that it is concise and effective, telling the story simply and clearly. Start at the beginning, and tell the story to the end. In court there are more formal procedures, but the court will order the day. You will have to take an oath and you will be directed as to what you may or may not bring into evidence. Hearsay cannot be admitted (unproven statements made by others not present) and you will be told this if you break this rule.

At either trial or arbitration there is a procedure of cross-examination: the defendant may question you, and you may question him. This should be a simple and straightforward matter – don't try to be Perry Mason. There is nothing so ghastly to watch as a rip-off performance from the American movies and it will not impress the judge or arbitrator.

Once the evidence has been presented, the judge or arbitrator will almost always make a judgment or award there and then. Rarely in debt cases is a reservation made to a later date, because rarely are there any great complications.

Appeal is restricted in the case of arbitration, but available in court trials. This can be costly and you must be sure that you have good grounds for an appeal. If it reaches this stage, then almost certainly legal advice must be sought.

- **The county courts can provide you with a very well written and detailed booklet entitled 'Small Claims in the County Court' (Form Ex 50). In addition, they can provide some outline documentation and will generally give useful guidance.**

# Index